SEXUALITY AND LOVE IN ARRANGED MARRIAGES IN INDIA: WHY ARRANGED MARRIAGES LAST

Wisdom House

SEXUALITY AND LOVE IN ARRANGED MARRIAGES IN INDIA: WHY ARRANGED MARRIAGES LAST

Vanitha Dayananda

Wisdom House
England· India· USA

First published in 2006 by
Wisdom House Publications Ltd.
Unique House,
I Dolly Lane,
Leeds, LS9 7NN
England
Tel: +44(0) 113 234 4466
Fax: +44(0) 113 234 4477
E-mail: editor@wisdomhouse.co.uk
Internet: www.wisdomhouse.co.uk

Simultaneously published in India by
Wisdom House Academic Publishers Pvt. Ltd.
126, Housing Board Colony,
Ambala Cantt. -133 001
India.
Tel: +91 171 2821237, 2821299
Fax: +91171 2821282
E-mail: wisdom_hap@yahoo.com
Internet: www.wisdomhouse.co.uk

Branch in USA:
9338 Sawtooth Way
SAN DIEGO,
CA 92129 USA.
Tel: (001) 858538-0611
Fax: (001) 858780-0521
(001) 619463-9402
E-mail: rajasue@aol.com

Our distribution links across the world.

First Edition: 2006

British Library Cataloguing in Publication Data
A catalogue record for this book is available from the British Library

Dayananda, Vanitha

Sexuality and Love in Arranged Marriages in India: Why Arranged Marriages Last

Library of Congress Cataloguing-in-Publication Data
A catalogue record for this book has been reauested.

ISBN 978-1-84290-185-4

Typeset in 10pt. Times New Roman by Wisdom House Typesetters.

This book is printed on an acid free paper.

Printed by : Vats Pac, B-98/1, Naraina Industrial Phase - I

New Delhi - 28, Ph. : 011-41410438, 41410439

CONTENTS

FOR MY SUCCESSFUL DAUGHTERS PRIYA AND SOUMYA

May they have good marriages by reconciling
the best of Arranged marriage and Romantic marriage.

ACKNOWLEDGEMENTS

The idea of exploring the most intimate thoughts of individuals regarding their sex lives and their marital lives seemed totally unrealistic when I conceived the grand plan of researching on sexuality and love in arranged marriages in India. The realization of this bold plan couldn't have been possible without the admirable cooperation, candor and encouragement of the participants of this study. To **all** of them, my immense gratitude and deep appreciation for having allowed a stranger like me to be a voyeur into "sancto sanctum" of your thoughts. In spite of your busy professional lives, you were generous with time and by saying, "don't hesitate to ask anything," "do you have any more questions?," you encouraged me to be an effective interviewer and showed your appreciation of my scholarship. The men and women of this study would not have been accessible to me without the efficient organization and competency of interview "arrangers". I am deeply indebted to the following people for their generous help, for their enormous consideration and sensitivity to my scholarship: Mrs. Indu Gajaraj, Mr. Jayanath Thomas, my late friend Mrs. Sheila Chandy, Mrs. Rathna Harish, Dr. Lakshmi Ragunandanan. I owe a special debt of gratitude to Professor Judy Brink, Department of Sociology and Anthropology, Lock Haven University, Lock Haven, U.S.A., for her immense support of my work, and for recognizing its importance. I appreciate her rigorous close scrutiny of my drafts and for her invaluable critique and suggestions. Thanks especially to a well-known Vedic scholar, Dr. Swamy Satyam in Bangalore, India who explained the complexities of Hinduism, the Hindu sacred rituals, and also provided English translation of the Sanskrit prayers and concepts. I gratefully acknowledge his fine contribution to my understanding of Hinduism. I would like to thank Professor Paul Amato, Head of the Department of Sociology, the Pennsylvania State University, University Park, U.S.A. for his professional encouragement and assistance. Thanks to Mrs. Audrey Barner, Department of English, the Pennsylvania State University for her meticulous proof reading. Special thanks to Professor Jeya Chandra, Department of Industrial and Manufacturing Engineering for providing computer assistance with patience. I appreciate the help provided by Mr. Kevin Wehnau, Ms. Alishia Urbanik and Ms. Jennifer Shultz of the Department of Sociology of the Pennsylvania State University in getting the manuscript ready for publication. I want to thank my generous friend Ms. Jean Alexander for the final scrutiny of the book and for her clever suggestions.

I also would like to recognize the valuable contributions of **all** the scholars whose work I have cited in my book. To the best of my knowledge, I have attributed the source of the literature to the authors. Nevertheless, there may be inadvertent mistakes of misquoting, inadequate citation, and misrepresentation. In case the authors find these mistakes, I extend my apologies to them.

Lastly, my deepest gratitude to the three scholars who played the final decisive role in making my aspiration a reality: Professor C.V. Venkatachalan, Retired Professor of Sociology, Academic Administrator National Education Society, National College, Bangalore, India, for his research assistance and for promoting my book for publication. Professor Vinay K. Malhotra, Principal, Markanda National College, Shahabad Markanda, Haryana, India, for reviewing my draft, for approving it and for endorsing it for publication by Wisdom House publications Ltd. Dr. Parvesh K. Chopra, Managing director, Wisdom House Publications Ltd., Leeds, England for accepting my work for publication. I truly appreciate the tremendous encouragement you have given me in publishing my book-it couldn't have been possible without you.

Preface

"How could you go to bed with a man or a woman who you do not love or have sexual attraction?," "what happens on the first night?," "How can you allow your parents to choose a marital partner for you?," Are there love and sexual attraction in arranged marriages ?" This book delves into these intriguing questions and more, that have mystified the Western society. Based on the lively intimate date of professional men and women, this work focuses on how and when love and sexual attractions begin in an arranged marriage, the couple "first night" experience, their sexual attitudes and practices, their definition of love.

A dominant majority of the participants of this study prefer arranged marriage, in spite of the fact they are modern, urban, university-educated professionals. Marital decision that hinges on shared sociocultural similarities leads eventually to marital compatibility is given as the compelling reason. Individuals may not know everything about each other's psychological aspects and other dimensions of the personalities of the partners they intend to marry, but yet they try to draw correct inferences, even if the premises are not comprehensive. It is said, "Life is the art of drawing sufficient conclusions from insufficient premises." An overwhelming majority also report that they have a good marriage; they reveal their can did thoughts on the positive and the negative aspects of their marriages, and the attributes of a good marriage. What the study has revealed is this: sexual attraction and love may not be absolutely essential as the criteria for choosing a marital partner and for a good marriage. Shared similarities and compatibilities, tenacious commitment, patient cultivation and construction of love and sexual attraction emerge as the decisive factors for a good marriage. The men and women display a unique strategy of "Reconciliation without Renunciation" — a fine skillful reconciliation of both traditional and modern ideas without completely renouncing either of them, in choosing a marital partner and living their marital lives.

There are six chapters in this book; the first chapter provides a general introduction to Indian Society and arranged marriage. The second chapter focuses on the comparison of the experiences of love and sexual attraction in **two** groups of individuals; **The Before -marriage Group** who developed love and sexual attraction **before** they got married and the **After-marriage Group**, who developed the same **after** they got married. The third chapter deals with the detailed explicit account and analysis of the "first night" experiences of **both** the groups. The fourth chapter deals with sexual attraction and compatibility of both the groups after a number of years of marriage. Factors that help foster sexual attraction and barriers to sexual attractions are both explored in this chapter. Companionate love the develops in a slow continuum after the marriage and respondents' definitions of love are discussed in the fifth chapter. The last chapter explains the reasons for the success of arranged marriage as well as the salient features of a good marriages along with the discussion of strengths and weaknesses of an arranged marriage.

Introduction

"How can you marry a person whom you do not love?"
"How could you go to bed with a man or a woman to whom you are not sexually attracted and you do not love or have sexual attraction?"
"Are people miserable in their marriages because there is no love or sexual attraction?"
"What happens on the first night after the marriage ceremony?"
"Isn't the first night a horrible experience for women?"
"Are women raped on the first night?"
"How can you allow your parents to arrange your marriage?" "Do parents force their children to marry against their own will?"
"How can your parents know what you are looking for in your future marital partner?"

These are some of the most frequent questions asked in the West about this strange, mysterious, long-established institution called "arranged marriage" in India.

Whereas men and women who had an arranged marriage often comment,

"I met him 17 days before the marriage... my parents went to his home to meet him and his parents, came back and told me I was getting engaged to him... I was young... I was excited about marriage because he was going to the U.S.A. There was no chance for me to think that I am sexually attracted to him. I liked him as a person, but no sexual attraction."

"My parents arranged the marriage for me... I knew my parents would

choose the right person for me... I value their judgment, their choice, their approval."

"My uncle and aunt arranged for me to meet her."

"I was not sexually attracted to him {or her} when we met"

"I was not in love with him {or her} before the marriage" "I knew him (or her) very briefly"

"My aunt introduced him to me... we met on the fourth of August... two hours after we met we decided to get married. We married 17 days after we met." "I had met him only two or three times before the marriage ceremony."

These comments suggest that love and sexual attraction do not necessarily play a paramount role in arranged marriages in India or in prospective marriage partners' decisions about marriage. "We decided to marry because we come from the same caste, class; we worship similar gods and godessess, we speak the same language, have the same traditions, life styles... we come from good families, we have educational compatibility"-these were the important factors in the decision to marry. These reactions reflect the importance of similarities and shared cultural experiences as the basis of marriage.

In addition to these, financial earnings of the potential suitor, especially the man; good health and sound mind; physical attractiveness and character above reproach, are stressed as valued resources (particularly for women) to qualify as a "suitable boy" and as a "suitable girl" for a marriage. It is not uncommon to hear from women, *"I was not sexually attracted to him," or "I didn't love him before the marriage, but I liked his educational qualifications and his good earnings. My parents and I knew he will make a good provider."* Marriages play an essential role in establishing the entire family's economic and social standing, even contributing to status aggrandizement and economic benefit. Hence, socio-economic resources are of great importance in the "marriage market" and to strike a marriage alliance. Compatibility and similarities in interests, attitudes, behavior and lifestyles of two potential marriage partners do not necessarily take precedence over socioeconomic similarities. Psychological profile of the potential partners and their psychological compatibilities are under emphasized.

Arranged marriage is more than an alliance between two young marriage partners, rather it is an alliance between two nuclear families and their extended families. *"Families marry each other!"* Potential marriage partners turned down marriage proposals because, *"She {or he} does not suit our family and can't adjust to our family."* Marriage is arranged within one's social networks; social networks determine and direct mate selection- *"my parents and uncle and aunt knew his family (or her family) before arranging the marriage."* Through marriages, long enduring connections between kinship groups are established, thus creating family stability, continuity and preserving the cohesiveness of the caste system. Mate selection is a systematic, rational, calculated decision making process based on deliberately constructed selection criteria. There is a cool, rational recognition of the fact marriage is for posterity.

In this preoccupation with the above desirable qualities and valued resources needed to strike a marriage alliance, other equally important factors essential for the success of marriage are often neglected or de-emphasized. The young couples are not usually asked by the parents and others "Are you sexually attracted to him?", "Do you find her sexually attractive?"- These comments would be considered outrageously inappropriate. The sexual attraction component of marriage is minimized. But yet it is important to note that individuals marry someone whom they "like." It is assumed by the arrangers that if two young healthy individuals with socioeconomic similarities marry and live together, *"somehow nature will take its course and they would become sexually attracted to each other and also become sexually compatible."* Perhaps Hindu culture has a deep Freudian understanding of human sexuality-sex is seen as a biological drive akin to hunger. So the elders may feel why make a big fuss talking about it ? Therefore, it is relevant to study how and when sexual attraction and love begins between marriage partners, their "First Night" experience, and their sexual attitudes and practices. Barriers to a healthy sex life and marriage, and the strengths and weaknesses of arranged marriages are equally important to study.

The present study, an analysis of love and sexuality in arranged marriages in India, is based on the data that I collected from in-depth interviews with 83 married Hindu men and women in Bangalore, who volunteered to be interviewed. Hence, the sample is not representative of neither the Indian society nor a particular caste. The sample is not restricted to one caste, but the respondents belong to many different castes. All the subjects have an endogamous marriage-married a member of their own caste. The sample consists of only urban, English-speaking, university educated individuals with diversified professional backgrounds such as university and school teaching, law, medicine, administration, banking, business, media and journalism. The data was mainly collected between 1992-94. Male respondents constitute 46% and female respondents 54% of the sample and also all of them had arranged marriages. The definition of arranged marriage should be clarified here. In educated middle class and upper middle classes, potential marriage partners are arranged to meet by the extended family members or social networks, with an option to accept or reject the potential partners.

Respondents belong to the various age groups of 21 to 49 years. Most of the men in the sample, 41% of them, belong to the age range of 31-45 years, and most of the women, 32% of them, belong to the same age group, and 4% of the male sample belongs to the age group of 20-30 years and 15% of the female sample belongs to the same group. It may be noted here, most of the men and women were in their twenties when they got married.

In order to have a reasonably balanced and inclusive gender view, both male and female subjects were sought for this study. Interviews were not conducted with married couples together, but only with the wife or husband of a couple. Although a majority of the respondents live in nuclear families, all of the respondents are closely connected and strongly associated with their extended families. In addition, many of the respondents had co-resided with their extended family members at one time or other. It is also quite common for extended family members to live with their married children. Contemporary Indian family structure, as discussed later, will shed more light on this issue.

Despite the fact that I started this research with a lot of trepidation about the sample, a few courageous pioneers were able to recruit other willing respondents, thus starting a snowball effect. The recruiters of the sample complied with my requirements of the sample and scouted respondents from their institutions without much difficulty. In-depth interviews were conducted in English and were taped in institutions and homes behind closed doors with each respondent, on a one-to-one basis. Time duration of interviews ranged from 60-90 minutes. Strict privacy was observed. At the beginning of the interview, I informed the respondents about the nature of my research study, the type of questions, and assured them of protecting the confidentiality of their interviews. I was pleasantly surprised that the interviewees were willing and enthusiastic about my research and allowed me to delve into their intimate experiences, thoughts and feelings. I did feel embarrassed a few times, when male respondents gave explicit descriptions of their sexual experiences. One man didn't understand the meaning of orgasm and he asked me for the meaning of it. The respondents were reminded that they were at liberty not to answer questions if they felt were too invasive. Only one respondent felt my questions were rather invasive and refused to answer some intimate questions. That person happened to be a female professor of sociology!

Even though there are innumerable impressive publications on Indian society from both Indian and Western scholars, the literature review conducted for this study reveals a dearth of in-depth, extensive empirical or ethnographic studies specifically on sexuality and love within arranged marriages among university educated professionals. In fact, Nair and John (1998), in their book, A Question of Silence, argue that there is a conspiracy of silence regarding sexuality in India. But, there have been some excellent studies and publications on sexuality and sexual behavior and attitudes in India. Kumar and Makwana (1991) deal with factors affecting sexual satisfaction. Kulhara and Avasthi

(1995) deal with sexual dysfunction, Kapur (1972) focuses on sex in marital maladjustment in India , Moni Nag (1996) deals with sexual behavior and AIDS in India. Gupta (1976) has dealt with love, arranged marriage and the Indian social structure. Levine *et al.* (1995) have explored love and marriage in eleven cultures including India as one of the studies. Dion and Dion (1993) have analyzed the role of cultural related factors-- individualism and collectivism in love and intimacy. The focus of recent publications on sexuality, love, desire, romance in India by Nair and John (1998); Puri (1999) Dwyer (2000); Bhattacharya (2002), is not primarily on "first night," love and sexuality, and factors related to the durability of arranged marriage among the urban, university educated male and female professionals. Nevertheless, Puri's excellent analysis deals with the personal narratives of gender identity and sexuality only among women in middle and upper-class. Although the subjects of my study include both men and women, women's accounts of marital sexual desire and sexual experience in this study, and their reaction to their extended family, and my analysis related to these issues have some similarities with Puri's publication.

There are also remarkable publications on marriage and family in India by Western and Indian scholars such as Seymour (1983, 1993,1999), Lamb (1997,2000)), Derné (1994, 1995), Raheja and Gold (1994), Roland (1988), Trawick (1992), Mines (1994), Uberoi (1993,1996), Sharma (2003). Although these publications, especially the exemplary contribution made by Kakar (1989,1990, 1992) have greatly benefited my own work, many of their subjects for research or focus of study have less specific application to my work on urban university educated men and women. Some of the publications mentioned here bring mainly western perspective to understanding the inscrutable nature of Indian society.

An unique feature of my study is the rich and authentic in-depth interviews with the male and female professionals about their marriages, their experiences of sexuality and love, and especially about their "first night" experience. This is an invaluable data. Individuals' experiences revealed "in their own words," sometimes in unabashed and uninhibited , explicit manner, add to the deeper understanding of the complexities of arranged marriage and the Indian culture. People's descriptions of their experiences in their own words put flesh and blood into the abstract nature of culture and theories of sociology, making it concrete and easily accessible for understanding. As Mines and Lamb (2002:4) put it, "culture is as culture does... And culture only does through active, living human beings. The discourses that are culture may come out not only in words, but also" in everyday activities. In addition to the interview excerpts of the subjects, I have also incorporated into this book, my own observations of the Indian society based on my socialization and experience of growing up in India. The vibrant everyday social comments that are mentioned here, are randomly made by characters in the social drama of Indian society; these "data" are cultural ideas and social directives that are very much part of the Indian socialization and experience. It has to be noted here that interview excerpts and everyday comments are italicized.

Another special feature about the subjects of this study needs to be highlighted; although they are urban, modern, university educated professionals, they reveal the forceful influence of cultural factors and social pressure on them, but at the same time they seem to have skillfully reconciled with some of the cultural constraints and social script.

In a sex study such as this, one is confronted with the question of whether respondents are telling the truth about their sex life and whether they would be honest in revealing information about their utmost intimate sexual behavior and thoughts. The respondents who volunteered themselves for the interviews are university educated professionals with appreciation for sociological research and realized the importance of their contribution to the research. In order to establish the validity of the interviews, interviewees were assured of confidentiality and privacy. Redundancy of questions and long, in-depth private interviews were used to increase the validity of this data. Furthermore, there was no motivation or reward to reveal information about their sex lives in a truthful or in a non-truthful manner-- their only motivation was to contribute to the knowledge of understanding of sexuality in arranged marriages. Since respondents revealed both negative and positive aspects of arranged marriage and their sexual behavior, I was reassured of the reliability and validity of the research.

This study is not a definitive study on sexuality within Indian arranged marriages as the cultural mind-boggling diversity of castes, religions, languages, class is a humbling experience for any scholar working on any Indian problem. I have come to realize that any comment, observation and analysis you make about Indian society could be both right and wrong. The Western readers may find inconsistencies in interviewees' views and my analysis; but it is unreasonable to expect consistency in a highly pluralistic society. It is my sincere attempt to barely scratch the surface of this complex problem of sexuality in arranged marriage. Readers may get a bird's eye view of how Hindu society shapes views on marriage, expectations of marriage partners, sexual practices, behavior and attitudes among one particular group of Indians, who are university educated, middle class and upper middle class. As mentioned earlier, since the respondents were not selected based on a coin-tossed random sampling, but on a voluntary basis, they do not represent one billion Indians.

It is my hope that this study may contribute to eliminate some of the weaknesses of the arranged marriage system. For Western readers, it may help in dispelling certain misconceptions about arranged marriages. In the West, marriages that are not based on romantic love and strong sexual attraction are somehow seen as unhappy and miserable marriages. It is my belief that societies, where the culture of divorce has become the norm, may find a few good tips and insights from the institution of arranged marriage. An overwhelming majority of respondents of this study report that they have a good marriage. Similarities of marital partners, compatibility, low-marital expectations, compromise and good understanding stand out as some of the reasons for a good marriage. Couples report that patient cultivation of love and sexual attraction, tolerance of each others' weaknesses and foibles, lower expectation of marriage have made their marriages successful. There is an unflinching faith in, *"it is the marriage that sustains love." "Make adjustment and somehow carry on your marriage," "you have to accept each other," "reconcile your differences," "act married"* the elders keep reminding the couples to strengthen marriages. Stoic acceptance of inevitable crisis in life and determination to cope with them, and the sustenance offered by the extended family are also seen as important elements. More than anything else a strong commitment to marriage is seen as the basis of a good marriage.

It is neither my intention to promote arranged marriage as a much superior system than romantic marriages nor it is my intention to recommend it. As in romantic marriages, there are inherent problems in the institution of arranged marriages. This study may offer a fresh perspective on how two total strangers with either some sexual attraction and love or no sexual attraction or love, negotiate their relationships, leading to what they consider as a successful and happy marriage. I have heavily depended on the voices of the respondents, as "their own words" can relate depth of their experiences, unaltered and unparalleled by my interpretation and my analysis. As a person born, raised, educated in India and married in the custom of arranged marriage, and furthermore as one who has lived and been educated in the west, I feel I may have brought a rare perspective; an insider's experience combined with an outsider's objectivity laced with sociological analysis.

The first chapter, **How does Indian society influence individuals view of arranged marriage?** deals with the objectives of Hindu marriage, sociological explanations of arranged marriage, and attitude towards romantic/love marriages. Sociological theories of mate selection and sex as applicable to arranged marriages are also discussed. In addition, the first chapter deals with sexual attitudes and beliefs of Hinduism and Hinduism's perspective on women and their sexuality.

The second chapter, **Is there any love or sexual attraction before the marriage ? Is love spontaneous or cultivated?** gives an analysis of the development of sexual attraction and love in both the **Before-Marriage Group** and the **After-Marriage Group.** The Before Group refers to respondents who had sexual attraction, love, physical intimacy and a period of acquaintance

before the wedding and the After Group refers to respondents who developed sexual attraction, love and intimacy **after** they got married. Furthermore, it explores how individuals condition their minds and deliberately cultivate and construct love and sexual attraction.

The third chapter, **What really happens on the "First night" or Does anything happen at all ?** deals with the "first night experiences of both the **"Before-Marriage Group"** and the **"After-Marriage Group."** The Before-Marriage Group's positive experience of the "first night" is attributed to their sexual attraction, presence of feelings of love, and a period of acquaintance before their marriage. Whereas, the After-Marriage Group's negative experience of the "first night" is related to lack of sexual attraction and feelings of love before marriage and also to the absence of an acquaintance period before the marriage. Moreover, the chapter also assesses the impact of Hindu rituals on the development of sexual attraction and enjoyment.

The sex lives of both the groups, after several or many years of marriage, are assessed in the fourth chapter, **Is there sexual satisfaction and compatibility in arranged marriages?** Reasons for sexual satisfaction and barriers to sexual satisfaction are also included in this chapter.

The fifth chapter deals with the questions: **How does love develop after the marriage? Is love missing in arranged marriage? What is the definition of love?** Love develops slowly and gradually in a continuum with several stages. Individuals varied definitions of love suggest that they have companionate love in their marriage.

The subject of the sixth chapter focuses on, **How and why arranged marriage lasts? What makes a Good marriage?** Factors related to marital satisfaction and a good marriage are analyzed here, with the inclusion of strengths and weaknesses of arranged marriage.

1

HOW DOES INDIAN SOCIETY INFLUENCE INDIVIDUALS VIEW OF MARRIAGE ?

Indian society is preoccupied with marriage. The most common, recurring annoying topic in conversations and in movies and in stories, is the ubiquitous topic of marriage. Chronic comments such as these are made:

"When are you marrying your son/daughter off?" "Have you begun to look for a suitable boy/suitable girl?," "We know a nice boy/girl," "What!!! no marriage yet?," "You better marry her off before she becomes old... she may not find a suitable boy." People quite often say: "Who is getting married to whom?" "To what caste does he/she belong?," "Which family is he or she from?," "He/she doesn't suit us." What does the boy do? How much and what are they giving? (meaning dowry and materialistic goods), Is the girl's character good ? Which family turned down the offer? Which family accepted the offer? How much are they spending on the wedding? How come she is not married...? maybe something is wrong."

It appears as though Indians live for marriage. It is the pivotal issue in social life and a central force in family and community life. Men and women who remain unmarried are seen as an aberration that may bring shame and dishonor to the parents.

In order to understand the beliefs, values, attitudes of the respondents of this study towards marriage, sex, and their sexual behavior, it is important to understand the socio-cultural foundation and framework of their thinking. It is not intended to ignore the diversity of religions in India and the diversity in approaches to love and marriage, but since Hinduism is the dominant force, and all the respondents are Hindus, much attention is given to this aspect. Although India is secular and pluralistic, most individuals shape their thinking and actions based on Hindu cultural patterns and religious beliefs, as noted in the interviews stated later. In this chapter, the following aspects are briefly examined: the objectives of Hindu marriage, the sociological framework for arranged marriage, the collectivistic nature of Indian society, the influence of family, views on romantic love, and sexual attitudes of Hinduism.

In contemporary India, traditions are slightly weakening as a result of impressive technological advancements and modernization; however, even the modern urban educated individuals seem to view the main aims of marriage as established by Hindu scriptures, the Vedas and moral-legal texts *dharmasartas,* with respect and importance. In addition, the great epics *Ramayana* and *Mahabharatha* are much venerated. The acceptance and justification of the custom of arranged marriage is also closely related to the great religious epic *Ramayana*. Hindus highly venerate, worship and try to emulate gods and goddess, *Rama* and *Sita*, the main characters of *Ramayana*, who had arranged marriages. The aims of Hindu marriage are anchored in the four aims of life in accordance with Hinduism; *dharma* (moral obligations in social, religious and cultural realms), *artha* (acquisition of wealth or economic and political activity), *kama* (pursuit of sexual pleasure or the life of the senses) and *moksha* (pursuit of salvation). As Zysk (2002:1) succinctly states, "This fourfold religious prescription characterizes the typical Hindu attitude toward life: all human activity is religious and sacred." The aims of Hindu marriage in order of importance are *dharma* (practice of religion and fulfillment of religious obligations, *praja* (progeny) and *rati* (sexual pleasure). Marriage is considered as a holy union for the performance of religious duties, for an unmarried male is forbidden to perform religious ceremonies. It is viewed as an ideal, a family duty and a social responsibility rather than as a promotion of self-interests and desires. *Praja*, the second aim of marriage is procreation of children, particularly a son who assures parents of salvation thorough performing the last rites after their death. Hindus believe in the three obligations; one to God, one to ancestors and one to the sages. A Hindu is not liberated from *pithru rana* (obligation to ancestors) until he procreates through marriage, specifically by bearing male progeny. Marriage defines manhood and femalehood and bestows adult status and its privileges on married people.

According to Meyer, (1995:146) Manu, an ancient prescriber of Hindu laws, makes marriage a requirement for a man "as his happiness in the next life depends upon a continuous line of male descendents who make periodical offering for the peace of his soul." Meyer comments that the first purpose of a woman is the bearing of offspring-- she achieves atonement and reconciliation through bearing a son... a son leads them (parents) to heaven...thus, marriage is necessary for both the sexes (1995:146). "The place of the male child in the family was so elevated, procreation was a duty in interests of the family and community" (Kapadia 1958). *Rati* (sexual pleasure) is the third aim of marriage and the last in the hierarchy of importance in marriage.

Kapadia (1958) points out that sex is one of the functions of marriage; it is given third place, indicating thereby it is the least desirable aim of marriage. Other scholars, such as K.M. Pannikar (1966), interprets the three aims of Hindu marriage by stating that the Hindu conception of a full life requires the balance of *dharma, artha and kama.* Neither *artha* nor *kama* should be neglected by giving a high priority to dharma, nor should dharma be neglected by pursuing only *artha* and *kama.* The laws of Manu state "*without dharma, kama and artha* become monsters."

The Hindu scriptures have delineated the life stages called *ashramas* for Hindus. Each life stage requires fulfillment of prescribed role expectations and moral obligations; *bramhacharya* (celibacy), *grihastha* (householder), *vanaprashta* (proceeding to the forest for the pursuit of higher learning), and *sanyasa* (renunciation of the world). Of all these life stages, the stage of the householder, attained by marriage is given enormous importance. It is the social and moral obligation (*dharma*) of the householder to perform sacrifices (presentation of gifts or acts to win favor) to gods and forefathers and to beget progeny. All these aims of marriage and obligations of life stages indicate the subordination of individual self-interest and self-gratification and emphasis on "social duty" as the basis of marriage. As Kapadia (1958) states, the moral obligations of *grihastha* reminds a man of the importance and ultimate good of living for others rather than for himself.

With the passing of the Hindu Marriage Act 1955, "the traditional aspect of marriage is now greatly changed and Hindu marriage today has assumed more or less the nature of a contract for the mutual benefit of the parties..." argues Basu (2001:36). Among the scholars and in the legal world, there is a debate about whether marriage under Hindu Law is a "contract" or a "sacrament" as discussed by Uberoi (1996). The argument seems to be settling on the stand that contractual nature of marriage is combined with the traditional belief and practice in the form of rituals; the traditionalists believe that the Hindu marriage is sacred and sacrament, irrevocable, permanent and inseparable by death. Marriage is not only necessary, but it is also a sacramental rebirth for women and an important *samskara* (ritual) to purify the body and soul. In order to stress the finality, irrevocable and permanent nature of marriage, to authenticate marriage and to fortify the true bond between the marriage partners, many sacred rites are performed with sacred mantras (prayers) from the *Rigveda.* Gupta (1976:79) comments that "marriage is considered as an ideal, a duty and a social responsibility ... rituals are role oriented, (such as the ones performed for the long, prosperous life of the husband), rather than person oriented (such as taking vows for the success of a person who is in love)." Shweder and Miller (1985:53) point out the importance of "organization of social roles that is fundamental" and "role-based obligations" are considered "salient" in Indian society. Vedic literature stresses the long, enduring nature of marriage by stating "the couple hopes to live a hundred autumns in a tender union of souls... with children and grandchildren playing around them and with these, they are filled with gladness" (Meyer, 1995:139). Married couples are prescribed and proscribed by Hindu moral-legal texts (*dharmasastras*) to follow the normative rules and expectations of marriage to achieve social harmony and honor in their marriages.

The Hindu marriage ceremony includes sacred religious rites performed by Brahaminic priests in front of Hindu deities and *homa* (sacred fire). All of the rites are essential to perform, to establish marriage as legal and to receive divine and social sanction. The two main sacred rites worth mentioning here are *laja homa* and *saptapadi.*

Laja homa- a rite which symbolizes fecundity and prosperity and also requires offering of ghee (clarified butter), rice and flowers to the burning fire- - the symbol of the God Agni. Satyam, a Vedic scholar explains the importance of the God *Agni* and the symbol of fire by stating that the God *Agni* is invoked in the marriage ceremony as the witness and registrar of marriage. Fire symbolizes eternal knowledge, vitality, purification, protection, energy and transformation. During this ritual the bride passes rice to the bridegroom and he offers it to the holy fire by repeating a Vedic mantra, which says,

"you are the source of my endless joy and the procreator of intelligent and cultured progeny for me" (Satyam 1995:25).

Saptapdi (the ritual of the seven steps)-- In this final and most important ritual in the marriage ceremony the edges of the clothing of the bride and bridegroom are tied together in a knot, symbolizing "the eternal knot", "the immortal tie" and "the inseparable union" of the couple. This "eternal knot", the bride and the groom are reminded by the priest, is a knot tied by God himself and to sever the knot (union) is a sin committed against God and will not be forgiven by him. As the groom leads his bride, they take seven steps together in unison around the holy fire, chanting one mantra for each step.

Saptapadi mantras express the seven principles for a happy marriage: to provide nourishing, good food in abundance; to attain physical, mental and spiritual strength; to gain wealth by righteous means; to acquire knowledge, happiness and harmony by mutual love and trust; to be blessed with strong and healthy progeny; to develop self-restraint and longevity; to establish true friendship and remain life-long companions in wedlock. After every circle around the fire, the groom assists the bride in placing her foot upon a stone. This ritual symbolizes the solid foundation upon which their marriage will be built. A prayer from the *Rigveda* recited at the wedding ceremony stresses the importance of long enduring commitment:

"Be my sakhi, we are sakhas
and let our sakhya continue.
Let this sakhya be not lost,
Don't give up my sakha.
Let us **will** *to be united.*
Loving each other,
let us share our tastes,
wishing well for each other,
sharing joy and contentment
let us unite our hope, ambition and souls"

Note: *sakhi, sakhya, sakha* mean partner or friend. *Sakhya* means union or friendship or partnership.

Another important aspect of the Hindu wedding ritual is the promise of the bridegroom to bride; he promises to perform and give *dharmache* (religious duty), *arthache* (earn money), *kamache* (sexual pleasure) and *nathicharami* (I won't leave you or violate you). "I *hold your hand for prosperity. May we live together for the whole life... I shall try my best to keep you ever happy with all my sweetness, submission and sacrifice for the development of our sweet home"* are some of the promises the bride makes to the bridegroom.

In all societies, wedding rituals are performed to indicate that marriage is an indestructible and an inseparable bond. But the motivation of Hindu wedding rituals extend beyond the interests of the couple who is marrying. That is, they are interested in maintaining the purity, continuity and integrity of the rigid caste system. Davis (1941;390) has identified the central issue, "by making marriage an eternal and indestructible union, the principle of caste itself is made eternal, indestructible, endogamous marriage being the heart of the caste order.

SOCIOLOGICAL FRAMEWORK FOR JUSTIFICATION OF ARRANGED MARRIAGE

What is impressive about the urban university educated professionals of this study is the attitude of **reconciliation without renunciation** of the ancient custom of arranged marriage; a compromising attitude that combines traditions with individual autonomy without completely yielding to either of them. Although forces of modernization and urbanization are resulting in mild relaxation of rigid traditional views toward mate selection; arranged marriage still remains the norm even among urban, university educated professionals. Mitter (1991:3), an American, notes an interesting approach to life among Indians; they think in terms of this "as well as that," rather than thinking as Westerners "this or that." Among the educated class, marriages are arranged in consultation with and in cooperation with prospective marital partners; they are active participants in the decision making process of marriage. However, in this study it is not surprising to find some university educated men and women who had subordinated their choice of their mate completely to their parents' desire and choice, but a majority of them made their marital choice in unison with their parents, while retaining their freedom of choice. *"We chose each other out of our free will; our parents did not force us into marriage"* are the common statements made during the interviews. Perhaps the privileged status of having university education with professional degrees gave them the justification and bargaining power to exercise their free will.

This is in agreement with Kolenda's (2003;398) statement that educated people in India have freedom of choice of their marital partners, but males have more choices than females and the educated women have "veto" power in selecting their marital partner. Seymour's (1999:212) longitudinal study in Bhubaneswar also supports the view that in spite of its transformation due to urbanization, modernization and education of women, even among the educated class, marriage continues to be arranged by parents, but with some participation by their adult children in selection of their partners. Derné's (1995) research on upper caste men in Banaras, indicates that college education did not alter their views toward arranged marriage. The tradition of arranged marriage challenges the argument that modernization and urbanization of societies leads to autonomous mate selection as economic resources are not family owned. What is phenomenal is even when economic resources are not family owned as in a feudal system, arranged marriages continue to be the norm because of the economic connections with the extended family. Furthermore, strong emotional associations and connections with extended family members encourage the continuation of this ancient custom.

Role of the Caste system, Family Structure, Collectivistic Nature of Indian Society in Arranged Marriage:

Gupta (1976:82-83) has identified the following three cultural factors responsible for the arranged marriage system. Other scholars views are in agreement with his views.

1. Arranged marriages are closely related with "closed system"-- that is, the Indian caste system is characterized by rigid hierarchy, ascribed status, occupation affiliation, ritual pollution, social distance. These attributes of a caste create individual and group identity, and formation of "in-group" and "out-group." In order to perpetuate, strengthen and maintain a caste, it is necessary to have endogamous marriages.

Of all the factors responsible for arranged marriage, a strong determination to preserve one's own caste purity stands out as a compelling reason. Hindus consider that it is *dharma* to marry a member from one's own caste. This idea can be found in the *Kamasutra* by Vatsayana; he states "that when a marriage to a virgin girl of the same caste is arranged according to the *sastras* (religious prescriptions), it results in duty (*dharma*)" (cited by Zysk 2002:15). An exogamous marriage is considered as "ruinous" to caste purity and a disgrace to family's name, lineage, honor and dignity. It is imperative to marry within one's caste. "Endogamy–i.e., marriage within the caste or sub-caste group, is one of the essential pillars of caste society... it functions to affirm and maintain caste status," argues Uberoi (1993:230). Basu (2001:27) discussing marriage in contemporary India states that the "Hindu ethos upholds marriage within one's own caste."

Dumont's views are in agreement with Gupta. Dumont (1970:59,60,197) has characterized the underlying principle of the caste system as "purity-impurity"; it is this principle that segregates and separates the castes from each other. "The purity of caste is to be found in blood, which is conceived not just as a substance, but as the basis of personal and family character... actions appropriate to caste and subcaste maintain the purity of caste" argues Harlan and Courtright (1995:6). The "insiders," the higher castes prevent the "outsiders," the lower castes from intermarriage with them, with the fear that it may pollute the purity, exclusivity and gene pool of their higher caste. Their actions are in accordance with their caste obligations. It may be reminded here that all the subjects of this study are married to a member of their own caste.

Kolenda (1978:6) argues that "persistence of caste in India, even among educated and modernized Indians is due to a kind of micro-community organization that the West does not have." Another principle of the caste system pointed out by Kolenda justifies arranged marriage. She believes that a caste is "considered a large scale descent-group"... "structured by a unilineal principle, (usually patrilineal) composed of a hierarchy of increasingly inclusive segments" (1978:7,8). She also promotes the argument that the arranged marriage "is essential to the preservation of the Indian caste system" (2003:358).

Perhaps a caveat needs to be mentioned here about the custom of arranged marriage; in some parts of India and among some castes, there are exogamous marriages. There are also innumerable subcastes. Each caste has its own "rules" about the exogamy and the endogamy nature of marriage, depending on their traditions and norms. Further discussion of this is beyond the realm of this book.

2. Gupta indicates that the cohesiveness, continuity and unity of the extended family are preserved by involving the elderly, experienced members

of the extended family in mate-selection decisions. Marriage and its survival are seen as a shared responsibility of parents and extended family. Whom an individual marries affects the status of the entire family, including extended family. Hence, such a monumental decision could not be left to the 'immature' decisions of the young people.

Closely associated with the consideration of caste in arranging a marriage is lineage. "The marriage arrangement becomes the primary context for sorting out where a particular family, lineage, and kin group ranks in relation to others" (Harlan & Courtright, 1995:5). Furthermore, Harlan stresses the importance that is given to family lineage while arranging marriage as it determines inherited character traits (1992:32).

3. Gupta also believes that the Indian social system in general is not keen on encouraging the development of individualism, economic security outside the family and the ideals of a nuclear family. The interdependency of the individual and the family (nuclear and extended) in matters of finance, housing, emotional support and physical care further reinforce the custom of arranged marriage. De Munck (1998) also argues that arranged marriages persist when economic resources are family controlled and it is promoted to avoid the loss of property through mate selection based on romantic love. Indian traditions and economic necessity promote reciprocal economic dependency; young people and even married couples depend on their extended family for financial help and in turn parents of married children continue to depend on children for financial help. As the government of India provides limited financial assistance to the elderly, children are their parents' source of social security, and they are also their health care-providers.

Rao and Rao (1982:16-17), citing other sources also point out the close relationship between arranged marriage and the joint family system. They argue that while the nuclear family system encourages romantic love, the joint family system promotes arranged marriage system as the latter has the following advantages to the social system: it helps in maintaining social stratification system in the society; promotes parental control over family members and preserves and transfers the ancestral line and property; it strengthens the kinship group and preserves the endogamous nature of marriage.

There are two schools of thought regarding the continuation and discontinuation of the joint family system due to modernization. One group of scholars argue that the joint family is disintegrating and being replaced by the nuclear family (for ex. Mehta 1973; Kapur 1965). Another group of scholars argue (for ex. Rao & Rao 1982; Ahuja 1993) that the joint family and its extended kinship ties and its basic characteristics remain intact, showing no major changes. But a more recent publication by Sharma (2003:8) establishes that the "joint family in its ideal form is in decline, evident only in one-third or less of the households.... " Joint family here is referring to a family with three or more generations sharing common residence, economic, social and ritual activities. It functions under one patriarchal or matriarchal authority with emphasis on filial and fraternal relationship. Indian society recognizes the advantages of the joint family system, as it establishes continuity of relations between generations and acts as a connecting link between the past, present and the future. It is also argued that due to the multilateral forces of industrialization, urbanization, education, and the economic independence of women, the traditional structure and authority of the joint family is weakening, but is not dead. Mines and Lamb (2002:115) note that their study and other scholars' studies also indicate the "transitional nature of families and gender systems, loosening of familial bonds of authority based upon age and gender hierarchies in favor of increased husband and wife intimacy.... "

The argument posed by Mukhopadhyay and Seymour (1994) further justifies the resiliency of the arranged marriage system. These scholars recognize that the Indian family structure has evolved over the years due to social changes, with increase in nucleated households or conjugal units. Nevertheless, patrifocal family structure and ideology survives with some modification and variation, as a "very prominent and culturally sanctioned system of ideal relationships and beliefs to which most Indians have been exposed and that provides a set of guidelines for social action." They note that the emergence of nucleated households can be compatible with the features of patrifocal family structure and ideology such as economic jointness, sons' responsibility for the elder family members and arranged marriage. The authors argue that the family structure and ideology create feelings of "obligation and responsibility" and "generates social pressure for conformity" (1994:7).

Ahuja (1993:37) points out that in modern India, "jointness" of family is not disintegrating: rather, the modern nuclear family continues to be "joint," meaning strongly connected with their primary kin parents and siblings in terms of "functioning." In his analysis of many sociological studies conducted on family from 1950 to 1980, decline in traditional joint family and change from sharing common residence to neolocal residence are some of the major changes Indian families have gone through. Other changes in the Indian family system are: increase in the number of "fissioned" families (sons prefer to have neolocal residence, but continue their traditional obligations to their parents); more equality of individuals, more equal status for women, joint decision of parents and children in mate selection, and weakening of traditional family norms are some of the other aspects.

Despite the changes the traditional nature of the joint family and patrifocal family structure have gone through, some core elements have remained stable, even for urban educated people, making the institution of family as the most reliable and resilient social institution. Most married children while living in neo local residence, continue to fulfill various obligations or *dharma* (moral duty) to their parents and elderly relatives. There is still a strong emotional attachment and respect for the extended family, suggesting a general satisfaction with the family environment. Even urban, educated individuals spend considerable amount of time with the extended family members, even though they may not live in a joint family structure. Seymour's (1999) study reveals that in spite of the education and economic independence of women, and changes in the patrifocal family structure and ideology, married daughters retain close ties with their extended family members. Spending an enormous amount of time with the members of a social group leads to strong pressure for conformity, states Collins (1988:114).

Even if many urban professionals do not live in a joint-family system, they are influenced by its ideology, which are according to Kapadia (1958), cooperative effort, authority of and respect to the elders, and observance of norms such as avoiding disagreement and argument with the elders. In addition, Kapadia (1966) points out the benefits of the joint family system to the individuals which are: economic help, emotional support, marital problem solvers and negotiators, socializing agents and care-takers of children.

The closely knit family, that is both the joint family and the nuclear, is the lynchpin around which individual's economic, emotional, cultural and social life revolves. Family ties are solidified and strengthened by its members involvement in family rituals of commemorating all the major life stages of individuals--birth, marriage, birth of a child and other important events in life. Furthermore, Hindus celebrate innumerable festivals that also reinforce long enduring family ties.

ROLE OF THE EXTENDED FAMILY:

Although the subjects of this study made their marital decision in unison with their parents and extended family members, nevertheless there is a mild, subtle, rather covert social pressure on individuals to choose a partner that parents and other elder family members think is the "suitable" person for them. Later on in this chapter, the section on **Socialization** will deal with how upbringing of Indian children plays an important role in arranged marriages.

It is not unusual for parents or elder relatives of the family to exercise their authority, power and will on marriageable children, by the virtue of formers' highest age status in the hierarchical structure of the family. They select the marital partner or influence whom their children ought to marry!. There is a general notion that the young people are immature and lack life experience, hence are not capable of determining their own good. This notion is in contradiction with the western Utilitarian philosophical theory, that individuals know themselves best and so they are best capable to determine their own good. In many technologically developing agrarian traditional societies, older people enjoy their filial piety, power, high status and importance given to them by the younger generation. Cowgill (1979) contends that as societies go through technological advancement, modernization and urbanization, the older people lose their high status. India may be a largely an agrarian society, but it is going through rapid technological advancement, urbanization, and modernization. Nevertheless these elements have not yet had a major impact on the high status of the older people.

Respect for the elders, compliance to their expectations and filial loyalty are stressed in Indian society-- violations of these norms would bring family criticisms and sanctions. Respondents of this study commented:

"We respect our parents wisdom, their experience... their judgment... we do not want to offend them or hurt them... they know what is good for us." "Whomever elders suggest we marry... we do not have much choice... but I have also rejected a few men that my parents suggested."

A female sports director of an institution commented,

"We don't have a special idea of an ideal man, we depend on our parents... we trust out parents judgment... I am lucky to have a good, very cooperative husband...I have no regrets... I am very happy. Even if I would have selected my own partner, I don't think I would have selected such a good partner."

In spite of prospective marriage partners were consulted by their parents before finalizing the selection of a suitable mate, they seem to acquiesce to parents' wishes, as noted in the comments of a bank manager such as this:

"I told my father any person you choose is suitable for me... you select anybody..., I'll adjust."

Another male professional says, *"I left everything to my parents' decision... and it is fine... I'll obey them... it is binding on my part."*

Such comments from urban professionals may be surprising, but they reflect the views of individuals in "duty based" society (Shweder and Miller, 1985:53). Derné's (1995) study on Hindu men revealed their concern about those who marry for love; they fear losing parental support and jeopardizing life in a joint family. The subjects of this study appear to reflect the views of people in collectivistic allocentric societies (allocentrics refer to individuals who center their interests and attention on others). For them parents' approval of their marital partner and conforming to parents' expectations is every bit important for their mutual harmonious relationship and well-being. Radhakrishnan and Chan (1997) reveal from their study that Indians are allocentric and the young people see their life goals are inseparable from their parents' life goals, while idiocentric Americans separate their goals from their parents'. Suh and Diener's study (1999) shows parental approval is much more important to allocentrics than for idiocentrics and also it is a source of well-being. According to Ratzlaff et.al (2000:40-41), idiocentrics endorse values, behaviors, attitudes common to individualistic/independent cultures, whereas, allocentrics endorse the same that are common to collectivistic/independent cultures.

The aforementioned comments from the subjects of this study regarding their marital choice may appear subservient and incongruous with their education and adult status. As stated earlier, a majority of them made their marital choice in cooperation with their parents choice, while exercising their own free will and yet some seemed to have compromised on their freedom of choice, while subordinating their choice to their parents' choice. What seems to surface here is the negotiation and compromise that goes on not only between individuals and their parents regarding their marital choice, but also the individuals are negotiating and compromising with their cultural expectations, practices and social pressures. They give the impression that **they** are defining or redefining or manipulating cultural norms or culturally constructing their own practice of arranged marriage. Individual desires regarding their marital choice are still considered important despite social pressures from their parents or elders in the family. Derné (1995:60,85) notes although men are strongly guided by social pressures in their married and family life, but yet their social pressures are complemented by "second languages" that gives importance to the individual (a term coined by Bellah et al 1985; Bailey 1991:214-215, that refers to contesting trends that are in contradiction with or actions that oppose the dominant cultural framework for understanding action). Many men in his study were aware of their own individual desires and allowed their desires to guide their action in spite of social pressure.

ROMANTIC LOVE AND THE COLLECTIVISTIC NATURE OF THE INDIAN SOCIETY, AND ITS ATTITUDE TOWARDS ROMANTIC LOVE.

"Before I do anything, I think twice, because I am afraid of my elders (parents, in-laws, grandparents, uncles and aunts)... I don't want them to think badly about me" says a successful pharmaceutical businessman.

The discussion on family in the above section suggests that Indian society is collectivistic in nature, in spite of rapid industrialization and urbanization. Based on longitudinal study in Bhubaneshwar, Seymour (1999) believes that it is too early to determine whether Indian society is transforming significantly from collectivistic to individualistic society, as a result of industrialization and urbanization. But she does recognize some positive changes in the status of women.

A dominant value profile of collectivistic Indian society is familism– a core belief of the joint family system continues to strongly prevail. Familism refers to a strong sense of WE feeling, surrendering one's aspirations and interests to family goals; considering family as the preeminent primary group; and obedience to patriarchal authority (Burgess et.al. 1963; Rao and Rao 1976). Rao and Rao (1982) findings suggest even nuclear family residents are as familistic in their orientation as joint family members and familism is highly pervasive even among college students, despite the influence of industrialization and urbanization.

The impact of collectivistic thinking and familism can be seen in individuals compromising on their independent thinking on mate selection. Dion & Dion (1993:53) quoting Hofstede (1984), states collectivistic societies have certain distinctive features which are different from individualistic societies. Collectivistic societies seem to stress the individual's loyalty to the group, the veto power and the superiority of the group. Moreover, they stress emotional dependence of individuals on groups, reduction of personal privacy and identity. Needs of the group, and the interdependence between individual and group are more important than the individual. "Marriage links two social groups... this is the reason why the choice of partners is rarely an individual matter" states Uberoi (1993:232).

Derné's study explores how the collectivistic framework for understanding action molds and constrains Hindu men. He states individual actions are not self-determined choices; rather they are the results of social pressure or reflection of the group that includes family, caste, religion. Furthermore, he indicates that the Hindu men feel uneasy without the guidance of family and society and they have "deep respect for the power of social pressure" (1995:46).

What also adds to the collectivistic thinking nature of Indian society is its holistic nature. Dumont (1970), the French anthropologist, argues that Indian society, unlike individualistic Western society, tends to be holistic. According to him, it sees society as a component of the cosmos, and societal members play their roles within the society, but without their well-defined identities. They see themselves as interdependent parts of society and as a member of stratified castes. This holistic notion may also promote the acceptance of arranged marriage.

Closely related to the notion of India being a collectivistic society is the notion that it is a "field society," a term coined by Ramanujan (1986:71) to emphasize the close interconnectedness of individuals with the group and the relational nature of Indian society. He explains "field society" in this manner:

"The field for a Hindu is predetermined in the sense that he comes into this world with the imprint of past karma. The home in which he is born, the nature of his parents, etc. is preordained. Since the field consists of many persons in the family, the individual's position is determined. Thus, the field creates a place for the individual. He is expected through his actions to maintain continuity from generation to generation. The field acts as a facilitator in presenting a model of behavior."

From the "field society" perspective, one can argue that individuals have a social responsibility to maintain generational continuity through arranged marriage, which is made possible through caste endogamous marriage. A compelling need of dependency on the group (the family), Ramanujan suggests, hinders personal choices. To opt for a "love marriage" based on personal choice of a marital partner, then can be seen as a defying act–an act to challenge the dependency on the family–the group, disrespecting the family's wishes. Some subjects of this study believe that their marital partner is determined by karma, which suggests again "field society" mentality.

Even among educated, urbanized Indians, the idea of romantic love as the **primary** reason for marriage is either opposed strongly or accepted with some reluctance or with lack of enthusiasm, depending on the degree of liberal thinking of parents. Seymour's (1999) study also indicates, that even among the educated class the idea of love marriage-the individual choice of a marital partner is distrusted, rather there is unwavering confidence that parents make a good choice of marital partners. Discussing the universals in Indian marriage, Kolenda (2003:359)) notes, "love between a man and woman is not considered a proper or good basis for marriage...". What disturbs parents about romantic love is that it may lead to marrying an "*outsider*" or "*he/she is not one of us.*" It is seen as the violation of the parents' choice regarding marriage partners. An "outsider" is a polluter of the "*clan charisma*" (a Weberian term. Charisma refers to the "divine quality" of a clan, which Weber thinks is a reason for emergence of castes).

There is also the fear of maladjustment of the son-in-law or especially daughter-in-law to the new family. Some fear, as a female government official put it, *"if the in-laws do not accept the love marriage, they'll ill-treat their daughter-in-law or son-in-law"*. There is better acceptance of romantic love marriages as long as it is religious and caste endogamous in nature. A male lawyer commenting about his marriage said,

"my marriage is both arranged and romantic, because I fell in love with a woman who belongs to our caste and the best part of it is that my parents approved of her!"

Parents appear to recognize the importance of love and intimacy in marriage. However, these emotional elements are not likely to be the decisive factors in the choice of marriage partners. Rather, it is believed that similarity of culture, caste and class are much more important factors. The interviewees of this study emphasize this and reveal their less positive or apprehensive attitudes towards romantic love marriage in the following excerpts:

"I don't think I could fall in love... it is difficult to understand everything about a person in a love marriage... people make impulsive decisions to marry in a love marriage and then sudden decisions to divorce."

"Real love develops slowly, gradually... romantic love is based on sex, after a few years, it fades away... the family breaks down... romantic love is not permanent."

"It is not necessary to have love before marriage... but mutual understanding is important... understanding his personality and how he thinks... similarity of family background is important... in the case of love (romantic) marriages... love is blind... they will come to reality after the marriage."

"In an arranged marriage, passion and love come later in a gradual process, whereas in a love marriage (romantic), love starts as a spark and then dies out... people begin to realize their incompatibilities after sexual attraction begins to wane away."

"If you fall in love , you are alone at times of problems... you don't have the backing of the family."

"In love marriage, only sex is on the mind; arranged marriage gives importance to other aspects."

"Sexual attraction can't be long last lasting... it is momentary."

One would like to assume that people with university education would appreciate individual autonomy and complete free will in marital partner selection, thus opting for "love" or romantic love marriages. But the subjects of this study see that romantic love and sexual attraction are transient, unstable, elusive and blinding and might exaggerate the strengths or minimize the weakness of a potential marriage partner or as Freud (1905) calls love blindness is "sexual overvaluation." Passionate love as a deciding factor or as a precondition for marriage decision is seen as irrational and irresponsible behavior. Romantic love is viewed as a self-interested act, which is disruptive to the cohesiveness and continuity of the caste system. It is felt as an impediment to the strong close ties of the family structure; it threatens the conformity tool of social pressure. It is seen as a barrier to individuals' allegiance and loyalty to the family. Moreover, individuals with their actions directed by group demands may not be willing to take the risk of alienating their family because "to act upon one's momentary judgment is to take an enormous cultural as well as personal risk. For most Hindus such action is unthinkable" Kakar (1981:37). By exaggerating the repercussions of "love" or romantic marriage, the social groups instill social fear in individuals. Derné (1995:72) finds "social fear as an exemplary, moral emotion that is the foundation of good behavior" in Indian society.

Hence, even urban educated people prefer to stick to the ancient tradition of arranged marriage, which has endured for centuries. Derné argues individuals depend on cultural understandings to guide and direct them when treading into unfamiliar actions. "Experience is a social and cognitive resource" that helps people to judge social norms critically (1995:143). Furthermore, he notes that the arranged marriage is justified by believing that love cannot be the basis for a successful marriage, a strategy to deal with the dilemma of arranged marriage. The experience of arranged marriage and the high survival rate of marriages of the older generation act as cultural dictates and guidance to the younger generation. Although a small percentage of people opt out for romantic marriage, nevertheless the dominant majority still prefer arranged marriage, as they have internalized the cultural dictates.

What is also at stake in an inter-caste and inter-religious "love" marriage is this–parents feel that if one of their children marries out of their caste, then it will have serious repercussions for their other unmarried children, especially for their daughters. *"Now that you are marrying out of caste, nobody will marry your sister... because of you, she'll remain unmarried."* In addition to this social embarrassment, as Kolenda (2003) comments, there is the possibility of family with intercaste/interreligious marriage accepting another marriage of the same sort by default, as other caste endogamous conscious families may refuse to give a bride or groom to such families who have mixed marriage. This is the main worry of parents. What is of real concern here is the "honor" of the family and the "shame" or "dishonor" a family member brings to the parents, extended family and to one's caste by marrying outside the caste.

A Brahmin business woman talking about her family's opposition to her marrying a non-Hindu, non-Brahmin, said:

"My father was not only deeply concerned about my sister not getting married because of my marrying outside the caste, but he was also worried about his losing his position as a board member in a Brahminic religious institution ...he also didn't approve the marriage of my brother to a non-Brahmin because my brother will not be able to do certain Brahminic rituals, as his bride is not a Brahmin." (According to Brahminic injunctions, both husband and wife should be Brahmins order to conduct the holy rituals.)

In addition to parents' concern about intercaste marriage of their children, the young couples who are planning to have self-arranged/romantic intercaste marriages fear the consequences of their decision. They are concerned about society stigmatizing them and their children. The fear that their children may have difficulty finding a suitable partner because they are the children of an intercaste couple is not far fetched.

An Indian professor of sociology considers romantic marriages as "*footpath*" (sidewalk) marriages, meaning men and women meet each other randomly on the sidewalk and allow their sexual attraction to rule their marriage decision. Potential marriage partners do not meet in sexual marketplaces (places to pick up sexual partners); rather they meet in marriage marketplaces (terms used by Laumann 2004, in his book "The Sexual Organization of the City"). Marriage marketplaces in India are usually relatives' weddings, places of Hindu festivals, parents' homes or at restaurants with parents or relatives present. Societal constraints and sexual self disciple prevent people from "falling in love" randomly. A male bank manager says:

"When we see a beautiful woman, we are attracted to her... but in Indian society, we can't enjoy (sexually) what we see... there are restrictions... we enjoy seeing her beauty and body... her way of walking... that's it!"

"Casteism represses sexual attraction."

There is a general feeling that romantic marriages based on emotions, but not based on similarities are unlikely to succeed. *"Love marriage is like a chewing gum... after sometime, the flavor is gone, then it becomes sticky and you are stuck"* says a male scientist. The western custom of dating many people and relationship breakups are seen by some as superficial, demeaning and devaluing of women.

"Sparks" and "vibes" do not rule the decision of marriage. Arranged marriage is basically a societal intervention into and control of the natural process of sexual attraction. Helen Fisher (1992) discussing the chemistry of love, points out the pivotal role played by phenylethylamine or PEA and other neurochemicals in infatuation or attraction. PEA, a natural amphetamine seems to stimulate the brain, causing infatuation or attraction.

Indian parents may not be aware of all this sophisticated brain chemistry, but one thing they know, young people are capable of making wrong unacceptable marital decisions based on their emotions. They intervene effectively and exercise their power and authority by imposing cultural expectations of whom to marry, thus controlling the influence of physiology.

Family elders and elder friends of the family take credit and responsibility for arranging marriages, take pride in saying how many marriages they have arranged, and for the happiness of the married couples (if and when marriages are happy !).

In societies with strong kinship networks and extended family ties, Goode (1959:40) argues, romantic love is seen as irrelevant and disastrous to marriage. This kind of thinking leads to the restriction of individual choice, and subordinating her/his interests to the extended family. Therefore, romantic love is not a precursor for marriage, rather a couple seeks to achieve "conjugal love" after the marriage and within the marriage.

Dion & Dion (1993) have pointed out in collectivistic societies married couples do not seem to seek their happiness, personal satisfaction and well-being mainly through psychological intimacy with their marriage partners, as may be the case in individualistic societies. Married people in India seek personal satisfaction and emotional intimacy from active involvements in many aspects of the lives of their extended family without depending heavily on spouses for personal happiness.

A married couple's schedule is filled with activities such as visiting sick relatives, and the new born baby and the mother; using "influence" to get a job, or school or university admissions; procuring goods and services for relatives, and most importantly arranging marriages! In addition, married couples, especially women, attend countless family functions such as seventh month ceremonies for the pregnant women, christening or naming ceremonies, "*mundan*" ceremonies (first hair-cut after the birth), "*upnayana*" (sacred thread ceremony) for the boys, funerals and the fourteenth day ceremony after the death, and, of course, attending innumerable weddings deflect excessive focus on spouses. Celebrations of countless Hindu festivals with *"pooja" (worship)* and special dinners offer couples personal satisfaction and emotional intimacy with the extended family. Hence, Indian society's limited emphasis on individualism that demands personal autonomy and psychological intimacy only with spouses may discourage individuals from opting for romantic love marriages.

After having taken the stand that Indian society is a collectivistic society that justifies arranged marriage, it is important to bring another opposite perspective. Mines challenges this collectivistic perspective and questions views which argue that individuals share collective identity of family and caste, compromising on their own autonomy. Based on his study in Tamil Nadu state in South India, he promotes the argument of "contextualized individual," meaning individuality of persons is recognized within the context of groups where they are known and within which they have a known set of statuses and roles. Contexts include the household, one's kin, and one's caste community..." (1994:21). As indicated earlier, the majority of subjects of this study decided to marry their marital partner based on their individual choice or as they put it, *"We chose each other out of free will, our parents didn't force us into marriage."* From Mines interpretation, subjects of this study have expressed their individuality, their personal interest, desires and preferences, but in the collective context of their family and caste. The competition in the marriage market among the educated class is based on an individual's educ^tion, professional training, occupational rank, income, reputation and other personal qualities in the **context** of his/her caste and family. The higher the individual qualifications and similarities, the higher the probability of a marriage alliance. Perhaps university educated subjects of this study have been able to achieve a harmony or a balance between their individual and group identity. A compromise between their utilitarian thinking and individual autonomy is achieved in their selection of a marital partner. That is, while it is important to select a marital partner who brings approval of the extended family and brings "greatest happiness to the greatest number," (extended family), the individuals also exercise self-interest and individual happiness.

An interesting aspect of collectivistic society is the use of gossip as kind of social "surveillance" strategy. The arrangers of marriage effectively use gossip in family functions and weddings not only as a social control, but also as an assessment or filtering system to find the right partner. They allow comments to float around and carefully register the reactions of people and use the information to their advantage. Comments such as these are quite common:

"He is our own caste, he suits our girl, fine... but what about his family's health and other things...?"; "I heard that the girl had a broken engagement... I wonder why ?"; "His brother is married for several years, but still there are no children... hm... ? !" "I believe the boy's mother is a little bit mentally unstable," "Have you heard about the suicide in that family?", "His father's eyes always look red...there is alcoholism in the family... she is very unhappy with her husband," "Have you noticed that the child in their family limps a bit and her eyes are slanted?", "I like their family... the girl is good, but she is bit too dark... not fair enough for our son." Another important question that is asked is, "Is the family in heavy debt ?" "I believe the family is in debt from head to toe" (meaning they are drowning in debt, hence unsuitable for marriage.

In conclusion, arranged marriages have their own distinct flavor, they are different from romantic marriages, yet there are some similarities. In romantic marriages, both in Western and Eastern societies, there is a common view that love primarily rules the decision of marriage, with importance also given to socio-cultural similarities. Pro-arranged marriage common view, argues that what is so called love is mainly sexual attraction, hence the stability of the marriage is suspicious. Glorification of love and idealization of a loved one are seen as spurious. But, as long as romantic love is based on similarities and compatibilities, marriage is likely to be successful in their opinion. There is also glorification and idealization in arranged marriages; the qualities and character of "a suitable boy or a girl" of parents choice are exaggerated. But as in romantic love, where an "irreplaceable love" is replaced by a substitute, in arranged marriage, "a suitable boy or a suitable girl" is quickly replaced by another "equally" suitable "nice" boy or girl in the marriage market. In both kinds of marriages, there is "shopping around."

SOCIALIZATION AND ITS INFLUENCE ON ARRANGED MARRIAGE

"Sleep next to the child, so that the child is not afraid of sleeping alone...; nurse the child on demand, don't put him on schedule; it is good to nurse the child at least up to two years old," advise mothers, mothers-in-law and grandmothers. A strong dependency of an individual on the family and extended family originates from infancy in India, leading to less independence in thinking and action in adult years in matters of marriage. Unlike the Western culture of child rearing that demands the separation of an infant's bedroom from the parents' bedroom, Indian infants, young children and even teenagers sleep in their parents' bedroom or in-between them. While lack of living space may be the reason for this, cultural reasons play a strong role, especially in not isolating an infant or a child from parents, particularly from the mother. This socialization process strengthens the closeness of parents and children, and the physical and emotional dependency on parents and extended family members. Kakar (1981), Roland (1988), Seymour (1983,1993,1999) and Kurtz (1992) and Trawick (1992) have analyzed socialization of infants and human interactions in Indian society, mainly within the Hindu joint family structure, using psychoanalytical perspective and ethnographic data. All these studies and observations reveal some striking features: gender differences in socialization; mothers giving disproportionate amount of time and attention to their infant sons; physical and emotional closeness between mothers and infants, especially sons; physical and emotional closeness between extended family female caretakers and the infants; unusual extended period of childhood and placing increased importance on interdependence, rather than independence; and most importantly group conformity. These aspects of socialization lend a strong explanation for arranged marriage. It may be noted here that publications on socialization in urban university educated class is rather limited.

Kakar (1981) has extensively psychoanalyzed Indian socialization, but reference to his excellent psychoanalysis is kept restricted in this study for the sake of relevancy. What is of relevance here is to focus on how socialization per se contributes to the acceptance of arranged marriage. Kakar emphasizes the establishment of close bond, attachment and physical intimacy between mothers and infants, especially between the mother and the infant son during socialization. He further points out the symbiotic relationship between individuals and the family that is created by the family fulfilling various needs of the individuals (1981:117). In his view, individuals accept their socio-environment with optimism and trust. Psychological identification of the individual with the family is so deeply imbedded that the loosening of the family bonds may produce psychological distress. He further comments, the welfare of others, subordination of one's interests to the wishes of others; obedience, respect and acceptance of authority of elder family members and their guidance are of paramount importance to Indians. These unique characteristics, Kakar argues, are due to "prolonged nurturing that leads to undeveloped ego" (Ibid., 107). Kakar further makes an interesting point about girls socialization; Indian girls are "born into a well-defined community of women" (Ibid., 61) who socialize the girls in domestic responsibilities and tasks, but also act as the girls' teachers and models. Hence one can argue that quite often older female members of the extended family influence younger women in their decision of marital partner, helping them to assess the qualities of a "suitable boy."

A number of scholars have emphasized the relational nature of the Indian concept of self that helps in understanding the individuals' acceptance and approval of arranged marriage. Mitter (1991) notes that "the individual in Hindu society is from the womb secured in a pattern of relationships...inculcated by one's kinfolk, reinforced by clan and community..." (1991:2). Roland's (1988) discussion of the Indian concept of self further helps in understanding the custom of arranged marriage. He suggests that the Indian conception of self is basically relational rather than autonomous and it is developed in the context of the hierarchical relationships within the extended family. An individual's self is influenced by characteristics of extended family that are: emotional interdependence, reciprocal demands for intimacy and support, and mutual caring. A high degree of empathy and sensitivity to other family members' needs and desires within the family structure also influence their self concept (cited in Dion & Dion, 1993:48-49). "I" is not the center of the universe, but "we" influences many of their decisions. There may be an ulterior motive in being relational; it may prevent social criticism and ostracism by elders in the family. Roland (1988:232-3) points out how physical closeness of mother and child "fosters a sense of self which is much more inclusive of we-ness." Another result of childrearing practice is the development of hypersensitivity to "what others say" – a cultural statement that is repeated. As Roland indicates, a central concern for Indians is "what is expected of them, (they) are acutely aware of how others are reacting to them. How one's behavior will be regarded by others..." (1988:252-3). In a slightly revised thinking, Roland (1989) recognizes that individuation can occur in spite of conformity to group expectations, but within the familial context. He also notes, unlike in western societies, there is a disconnection between separation and individuation in the functioning of Indian familial self. Meaning family members can maintain their individuality, but their definition of their individuality may not be connected with separation from family members and establishing their autonomy.

Seymour's study also describes the enormous physical closeness that mothers and other extended family caregivers had with the infants and their providing attention to all the demands of the infants. In addition, her studies show although mothers did not give consistent and constant attention, they fed their infants whenever they demanded and continued to bathe, dress, and hand-feed children until they were ten years old (1983:135,1993:59). In her earlier study (1971), she makes an important statement about Indian socialization. She claims that Hindu child rearing practices insist on children's renunciation of their independence, self-interests, wishes and desires in order to preserve the cohesion of joint or extended family. In agreement with Kakar (1981), she also suggests "prolonging a child's physical dependence on others "creates" a sense of interdependence in a society that does not value independence...." (1993:59).

An unique feature of the socialization of children in India is the presence of multiple caregivers-members of the extended family who provide childcare in addition to the care given by their mothers. Sharma's (2003:40,41) study indicates, "multiple care givers are active in the first and second years, their contribution to childcare is more profound during the latter half of the second year and the third year." He notes that care giving by the extended family members "increased as children became increasingly mobile, verbal and interpersonal." Kurtz (1992:144) promotes the idea that multiple caretakers or multiple mothers that individuals have during their childhood teach them to abandon their selfish preoccupation with their natural mother and make them realize that care is given to them by a group of caretakers. This in turn leads to the "self becomes a group self" and to the awareness that they are cared for by the group, thus making them less independent, less self-interested and more sensitive to the expectations and demands of the group. Trawick (1992:242-243) uses an unique term, "de individuation" to describe how in human interactions in a tightly knit South Indian family, the idea of development of "self" or individual autonomy is discouraged, but emotional attachment to the group is encouraged.

What is of monumental importance to the social development of children in Hindu society is the role of Hindu rituals (*samskaras*), through which children are introduced to the basic beliefs of Hinduism and are integrated into the society. Parents, extended family, friends and community are actively involved in the celebration of these rituals. They bestow recognition, praise and gifts on the children on the day of the rituals. Children go through various rituals according to their cognitive and social development, but the ritual customs and their names may vary from caste to caste. They first start with the religious ritual of naming ceremony; followed by first outing ceremony, that consists of "looking at the sun" "looking at the moon"; then "rice" ceremony (weaning from breast milk and introduction of solid food to the child's diet); "ritual of tonsure", a child is taken to the temple to shave his baby hair and offer it to the goddess of family's choice. Brahmin boys in the age group of five to seven years old have additional ritual of "thread ceremony," also called "second birth ritual." This rite of passage gives him legitimacy to perform sacred rituals and gives him adult status to join the "exclusive" club of adult men.

Sharma argues that the purpose of these rituals is to guide the development of children within the intricacies of family and community relationships and to facilitate anchoring their emerging self-identity in parental, familial and community interactions. Moreover, the social network "predisposes children to develop not simply some kind of homogeneous group self, but rather socially embedded relational self that includes affective identifications and representations of multiple caregivers" (2003:39). These profound latent functions of rituals and their influence on social development of children prepares their minds to accept arranged marriage later on in their lives.

As alluded to earlier, the majority of the subjects of this study made free choice of their marital partners in consultation and in cooperation with their parents. Perhaps this can be attributed to their socialization, where as members of educated class they might have developed some individual autonomy, self-determination and self-will. Data on the socialization of children within educated class is rather limited. Nevertheless, Seymour (1999:270) has noted in her study, as a result of change in child rearing practices due to societal changes, middle and upper-status children were developing self-reliance, less interdependence and less group conformity. But the subjects of this study still had the need or were under covert social pressure to acquiesce to their parents' or to the family elders' expectations of their marital partners.

As indicated earlier, conformity to the elders' expectations, filial loyalty and respect for the elderly are common cultural dictates in the hierarchy conscious Indian society. An important aspect of the Indian socialization is the inculcation into children's consciousness, the cultural ideas of "dharma" (moral obligation), "respect," "duty," "obedience," "gratitude," "service," "devotion" to the parents and to the elderly relatives. In the voices of the subjects of this study, these cultural ideals are echoed. Children are taught how to be deferential to the elderly in conduct, speech, and in important decisions. It is socially imperative to use polite, respectful, formal language with the elders. Young people are expected to show reverence and humility by touching the elders feet on important occasions, position their folded hands on their chest and slightly bow their heads when they greet them. Crossing one leg on the other, pointing one's feet towards the elderly, sitting in a chair while the elders are standing, speaking to them and dressing in a disrespectful manner are violations of acceptable conduct that would result in mild punishment.

Cultural practices and ideas, which are internalized during the socialization later justifies the custom of arranged marriage. In agreement with many scholars, Shukla (1987) and Mines (1988) also note that individuals' independent beliefs, autonomous thinking and actions tend to be stifled by social pressure to conform to the family's expectations, and by pressure to maintain harmony and cohesiveness of the family. As noted in the interview excerpts below, people are likely to abide by their parents' choice of marital partners as an obligation to them and to show their indebtedness to them for having performed all their parental obligations diligently. Family relations is based on what Vatuk (1990;66) calls "long-term intergenerational reciprocity." Lamb (2000:46,47) in agreement with Vatuk and with this study, describes "family relations as entailing long term bonds of reciprocal indebtedness extending throughout life and even after death." By fulfilling all the parental obligations to children: providing physical care, education, socialization and performing the religious rites, parents create in them "a tremendous moral debt," or dharma, so that children reciprocate parents' obligations in their old age.

What the following excerpts from the interviews of this study reveal are the echoes of socialization; how the inseparable, reciprocal connections exist between parents and adult children, how the individuals yield to social pressures and how their social action is in accordance with social script. It was quite common to hear that the primary reason for marriage;

"was not love or sexual attraction, but to marry someone who will take care of the parents and adjust themselves to the new responsibility of caring for the elders, financially and physically"

A prominent male scientist revealed;

"Whether I am sexually attracted to my future wife didn't even come to my mind... I concentrated on my principle objectives of life... I asked my future bride whether she can cope with taking care of my parents. It is the moral duty of children to take care of their parents in old age... When I was a child, they didn't pay somebody to take care of me. So, how can I ask somebody to take care of my parents."

A female professor commented,

"When we met each other we were not thinking about sexual attraction for each other, I just wanted to know about his thinking, his views, his family... whether I can adjust myself to his family."

"I decided to marry her," says a program executive, "because there was compatibility of the families... her family is a learned good family, all the members of my family accepted her."

"Sandwiched women" take responsibility not only for their own nuclear family, but also for their aging in-laws, in addition to their professional responsibilities. Parents prefer potential brides for their sons who are sensitive, caring and respectful of the elderly-*"We want a girl who will take care of us in our old age."*

Who really has a great influence on the marital decisions of their sons is, of course, mothers ! There is a Bengali Hindu wedding ritual that is described by Lamb (2000:57) that captures the close relationship of mother and son. Before a bridegroom departs for his bride's home for the wedding ceremony, the mother washes his feet with water, milk and turmeric (a spice with medicinal quality) and wipes his feet. Then, she "is supposed to have her son symbolically nurse at her breast" to signify that her work toward him is over and from now on his wife will assume the mother's responsibility for him. While this custom may appear outrageous, it suggests not only the excessive dependency of men on their mothers, but later on they expect their wives to be like their mothers. Observing Indian men and the disproportionate attention given to them by their mothers and other female relatives, Mitter notes "After all, men are just grown up little boys, like the child-god Krishna, who rely on a mother to look after them" (1991;106).

One would expect that Indian urbanized university educated professional men would be less influenced by their mothers on decisions of marital partners. But, Indian mothers play a decisive role in the mate selection of their children, particularly influencing their sons choice of brides. Sons seem to acquiesce to their mother's wishes. "Mother knows best" when it comes to selecting a suitable girl, as it quietly assures men of virgin brides; *"she is chosen by my mother, so I didn't worry about her virginity"* says a transportation executive of this study.

Gore's (1968:178) research findings on closeness of relations of a man with his wife and mother, reveal that highly educated urban men are equally close to their mother and wife. "In the traditional family, relation with mother is more primal than with a wife." But many urban professional university-educated men in this study show a strong primal bond with their mothers, in spite of the fact they are not in rural areas in a traditional joint family system. It may sound like a far-fetched idea, but Indian sons' devotion to their mothers has semblance to Catholic societies devotion to Mother Mary. Here is how several professional men of this study describe their relations with their mothers:

"I love my mother... when my mother said I should marry her... I decided to do so... I started loving my future wife and began to have sexual attraction towards her."

"Before my mother died, she had expressed her wish that I should marry her (my present wife). I carried out her wish."

"I had entrusted the responsibility of finding a girl entirely to my mother."

Men without any fear of being labeled as "moma's boy," admit such close relationship with their mothers. The most preferred status that mothers bestow on their sons and their indulgence in them sometimes circumscribes their independence. An excessive dependency on mothers starts in their childhood. As indicated earlier, it is not uncommon to see boys sleep with their mothers until they are 5 years old or even older. Mothers are especially diligent about the protein intake of their infant sons for their intellectual and physical development. A successful cardiologist emotionally and fondly reminisced about his mother, *"My mother used to put ghee (clarified butter) into milk and feed me when I was a child and a teenager."* A professor of agricultural science stated *"My mother used to collect the cream after boiling the milk and give it to me as a child... that is why I am successful now !!"*

As already stated, Kakar (1992) maintains that mothers are the primary caregivers and they have a close bond with their sons, unlike their fathers who play a less important role in childcare. But a few other studies, such as Roopnarine *et.al* (1990, 1992) and Sharma (1998), challenge Kakar's argument. They observed fathers in urban, educated, dual-career families are active participants in child rearing and exhibited emotional and physical closeness with their children. In Kakar's book *The Inner World*, a psychoanalytic study of Indian childhood, argues that Indian mothers are emotionally attached to their sons as a reaction to the emotional distance they feel in an arranged marriage and constraints put on husband and wife intimacy (1981). He claims mothers tend to see their son/s "as a kind of savior given the heavy cultural emphasis on the bearing and raising of sons, the traditional goal for a Hindu woman" (1981:88). Sons are their caretakers in their old age and act as a source of built-in social/financial security, especially after their husbands pass away. Therefore, it becomes a form of coping strategy to demand devotion, attention and obedience from their sons.

A female engineer said, *"I turned down a proposal from a man whom I liked mainly because of his mother... when they came to see me, his mother was holding his hand... I quickly foresaw what was coming if I had married him... his mother would have taken over our lives!"* As it will be noted later, mothers also become a source of marital conflict and "kill joys" of sexual pleasure of their sons.

Although subservient behavior of women is an ideal in the domestic arena, older women, by virtue of their age status, have considerable domestic power and authority in matters that are related to marriage and the marital relationship of their children. Older women seem to feel a sense of personal satisfaction and pride as their power lost outside the home is compensated by control over children, sons-in-law, daughters-in-law and grandchildren.

Paramount in the Indian marriage is the belief in karma (one's present life situation is predetermined by deeds of the past)-- one of the basic principles of Hinduism also plays a role in the choosing of a marriage partner; individuals tend to think it is their fate to marry a particular person, because that person is predestined by their actions in their previous life, hence that person is the right person to marry and love. This stoic acceptance of life situation is likely to create passivity and an uncritical acceptance of arranged marriage. Failure and success of marriage are attributed to karma... *"My marriage turned out to be happy because our horoscopes matched and it was all my karma"* is not uncommon comment. A professor of physics, commenting on his unhappy marriage with sexual incompatibility said, "*Even though I am a scientist...I hate to admit it... my karma has something to do with this !*"

SOCIOLOGICAL THEORIES OF MATE SELECTION AND SEXUALITY AS APPLICABLE TO ARRANGED MARRIAGES IN INDIA: A brief analysis.

The analysis of the present study is rooted in the sociological perspective that includes the following sociological assumptions: individuals' mate selection and expression of sexuality are strongly influenced and constrained by societal rules and values. The social rules and norms that direct the individuals' behavior are interconnected with the basic societal institutions of marriage and family, religion and the caste system. Furthermore, it is the pervasive influence of culture and its scripts and the individuals reaction to them that define the mate selection and sexual behavior.

The institution of arranged marriage is strongly rooted on the principle– the greater the similarity between a couple in religion, caste, class, genes, education, language, and family background; the greater the success of their marriage and greater the marital satisfaction. Nevertheless, there are certain castes, especially in North India, that promote exogamous marriages; that is, individuals marry outside their castes, but castes that are compatible with and complement them. In this study, all the respondents' marriages are endogamous in nature; especially in the area of religion, caste, class, family background and language; but the education level varied between spouses. Why is there so much emphasis on similarity? Because it facilitates, as they argue, marital adjustment and lack of it leads to "marital misery," "marital disharmony," "marital conflict," "breakdown of the family," "unhappiness of the children." Similarity also leads to the perpetuation of lineage and religion, caste and the class system and good quality genes.

Nobody can escape the enormous power of socialization. As the **Social Learning Theory** argues, children learn behavior through imitation, observation and reinforcement. Living in a culture of arranged marriage, young people come to accept it as the norm. It has been promoted and perpetuated for generations. Individuals learn to imitate and observe their parents and relatives pattern of arranged marriage. Furthermore, young people who comply with the parents choice of suitable partner are rewarded. Family's economic privileges and property are bestowed, while individuals who opt for "love marriage" may encounter family opposition and loss of family privileges. "I don't want to hurt my parents or disobey them or embarrass them" are the concerns of the younger people. Thus, we also see **Social Control Theory** in operation.

As noted earlier, marriage is more than an union of two individuals. Rather, it is an union of two families. An individual's decision to marry is made in the context and interest of the entire family or household–the crux of the **New Household Economics** view. It is a collective decision for the welfare of the entire family.

The idea that a suitable boy or a girl is "One of us" is the sole predictor of marriage settlement. Perhaps the best sociological theory that can explain mate selection in India among the educated urban class, is the **COMPATIBILITY**

THEORY of mate selection, which assumes mate selection is based on **similarities** of social status, race, education, family background, lineage, religion and ethnicity. It is quite obvious that Indian society, with its strict societal norms and expectations, has imposed rigid cultural barriers that restrict the choice of marriage partners to within endogamous groups or to compatible castes. An overwhelming majority of the respondents of this study are married within their own caste, religion and class; they have similar or compatible education and profession.

Although physical attractiveness of a man is not the main criterion in choosing a marital partner, nevertheless the arrangers do pay attention to the physical similarities of potential marital partners. The physical similarities variables include; skin color, attractiveness, age and height. Two individuals' social similarities are enhanced by physical similarities. And when this kind of matching exists, the arrangers and the relatives feel, *"Isn't it a perfect match!" "They look beautiful together," "Both of them are tall" "Both of them short," "Both of them are fair." "Both of them dark."* In case they can't arrange individuals with physical similarities, it is compensated by other more important factors. In most Indian marriages, men are about five to six years older than women, thus men's economic resources and education are compensated by women's younger age.

Although nobody overtly mentions the role of genetic similarity in arranged marriage, attention is given to diseases in the family of the suitors, as well as physical deformity or mental impairment or illness and infertility. The mediators of a marriage covertly do the homework on the families and lineage of the suitors in order to extract the "inside" information. Caste and class endogamy, especially among the upper caste and upper class, promotes genetic similarity between couples. Genetic similarities between couples have certain advantages as pointed out by Ada Lumpert (1997), an evolutionary psychologist. Based on many studies, she points out the greater the genetic similarity, the greater the fertility rates, the greater the intelligence and the health of children. Furthermore, she adds genetically similar couples have greater marital harmony and stability.

Most of the respondents did not mention shared interests as the basis of their marriage. Perhaps, it is assumed people with similar socio-cultural background also have similar interests. Nevertheless, comments such as these are reported in this study:

"He is a great lover of music... I wanted that type of man... I wouldn't have married a person who would have not appreciated and encouraged my interest in music... I take more pleasure in music than sex... he is very much interested in music like me."

"We were attracted to each other by our ideas and interests... we like music, literature."

Arranged marriage could also be explained by **THE SOCIAL EXCHANGE THEORY** (Homans, 1961; Murstein, 1980), which assumes mate selection is based on cost/benefit analysis. According to Homans and Murstein, individuals seek marital partners who will maximize their rewards or assets from the marriage and the choice of a partner is influenced by the perception that both their assets and liabilities are approximately equivalent to one's own assets and liabilities. In Indian arranged marriages, since the personal emotions of the prospective partners are not given serious consideration, parents and the extended family assess the costs and rewards of a marriage alliance; if the assets of a marriage alliance are high and liabilities are low, marriage plans are likely to materialize. In this highly competitive marriage market, negotiators (parents or relatives) of marriage alliance are "shopping around" within their social networks for the best deal! The materialistic nature of arranged marriages seem to reflect the influence of capitalism.

Mediators for the prospective bridegroom display their "suitable boys" valued resources-- education, profession, income, family background, lineage, caste and show their willingness to trade these for "suitable girls" valued resources-- education, occupation, income, good family name, good looks, fair skin, good moral character (meaning she should be a virgin) and domestic capabilities.

If the negotiators or the mediators see assets and liabilities of prospective mates are **roughly** equivalent and if they see each other's personal resources maximize prospective mates and their family's rewards from the marriage, a marriage alliance is struck. If not, the process continues until they could find another marriage alliance that has more rewards than costs. In general, even among upper classes, eligible men have a wider marriage market than eligible women.

A "fair girl" or a girl with "wheat complexion" has higher demand than dark-skinned girls in the color sensitive Indian society; so much so that "Fair and Lovely," and "Fair Glow" – skin lightening skin creams may have become a billion dollar industry in India. Fair skin is more desirable than dark skin, as the goddesses *Parvathi, Sita, Saraswathi* are fair and beautiful whereas Kali, the goddess with frightening looks is dark. In the marriage market, eligible bachelors and their mothers are particular about "fair girl," but this is compromised by *"dark, but attractive face."* A businessman talked about his compromise, *"I was looking for a fair girl, but she was dark... but I was attracted to her attractive face."* While light skin is preferable, nevertheless, a compromise is made by professional men, if the women's professional qualifications compensate their dark skin. *"She may be dark, but she is a doctor."*

The personal resources of prospective mates need not match exactly, rather the match may be complementary– a man matches his high economic status, education, profession, abilities as a good provider and his older age with a woman's low education, low economic status, low income, younger age, fair skin, good character, physical attractiveness and domestic capabilities. This kind of marriage alliance is complementary in nature; one's inadequacy is compromised or complemented by the other's. In this sense, the institution of arranged marriage is highly beneficial for men and women who have certain disadvantages, physical or intellectual; with effective intervention and negotiation of their family, they have a chance to marry. The same people may have difficulty surviving the competition of marriage market on their own. A man who has economic resources but is short, fat, and has other physical mild deformities has a higher chance to marry, than a woman with the same physical unattractiveness or deformities.

Generally speaking, in the marital partner selection among middle class and upper middle class Indians, males have higher education and economic resources than females and in many cases, both males and females have equal professional qualifications and incomes. But in cases where females have higher professional qualification and income than males, the females have to make a compromise. They experience hypogamy. A female physician reported that she married a man with lower qualification than her because of the concern that she may not find a suitable partner. In circumstances where females have higher qualification and higher income potential than males, parents try to inflate their son's credentials. *"Isn't he a man ?!"* - in their grading system, their child being a male itself is a higher credential than a female, in spite of the fact a female may have higher credentials than a male.

Despite the fact that most individuals marry within their own caste in an arranged marriage, the caste rules and norms dictate that subcaste members may marry each other as long as their castes are complementary in nature, even though they belong to two different castes. For example, a man who is a *Smartha Brahmin* may marry a woman who is a *Madhva Brahmin*; the two subcastes are complementary in nature, but different. Moreover, both the castes are the subcastes of the Brahmin caste.

Such is the rational and calculated approach to marriage, parents formulate their own "grading system" or numerical ranking system of suitors; the higher the similarities and assets, higher the grade or score and higher the possibility of marriage. Parents or negotiators remind young people, *"You can't expect number 10... somehow adjust."* When the marriage alliance is struck, they announce, *"The marriage is settled!"* It is more common to hear, *"He approved her or accepted her,"* rather than vice versa. When an intended alliance or engagement breaks, it is more often *"the boy's family"* or the *"the boy"* who decides to renege on their agreement. Arranging marriages benefit the mediators; they achieve recognition, higher status and importance.

Whose interests do Indian marriage customs serve ?

Well, as the **Social Conflict theorists** would argue, of course they serve the interests of the castes, the upper classes, the extended families and the young couples, so that they can maintain power over economic resources and transfer them to their progeny. Traditional customs of arranged marriage perpetuate the rigidity of the caste system. Marriage is institutionalized to preserve the purity of the castes. As Davis (1941:388) commented, "The more rigid the stratification, the stringent the endogamy." Individuals have to marry individuals like themselves; *"he/she is one of us," "he/she belongs to us"* are recurring comments that reflect the individuals desire to preserve the caste identity and integrity. Although young couples from educated families and upper classes have freedom of choice in marriage, nevertheless they are expected by societal norms to surrender their freedom of choice to the elders.

Not all castes and families have the custom of dowry, but in families where dowry is accepted and asked, parents with a highly qualified son with enormous economic resources maximize the dowry value of their son, while bride's family negotiate for minimizing the dowry cost. Parents have authority over mate selection because of dowry. Through skillful mediators of marriage, an alliance is struck between families with comparable social and economic status; both families try to enhance their social prestige by marrying into a socially reputable family. Although the custom of dowry, a function of arranged marriage is meant to give an initial economic base and security to the newly married couple and to the financial security of the bride, it is considered by progressive modern thinkers as an exploitative and dangerous social evil.

It appears as though "business" of Indian marriages is business and potential suitors are commodities who could be exchanged at a high value in the marriage market depending on their value. A driving force behind arranged marriage is really the "E" factor – economic factor, to ensure that property and materialistic privileges are passed on to the deserving candidate of the same caste and with the right family background and ties. Marriage is viewed as an opportunity to advance economically or preserve the economic and the caste status quo.

A divorced professional woman (not a subject of this study) criticizing the "commodification" nature of arranged marriages talked about how her extended family tried to break her sister's love relationship with a man outside their caste and arrange marriage for her with the professional woman's divorced husband. They felt, *"this could heal the fractured relationship and bitterness between the families."* Family's interests and reputation override the individual's interests.

This commodification of marriage is also reflected in the language of the marriage market:

"The boy came from America and I had lined up six girls for him to see. After interviewing all of them, he chose her; he rejected others."

"The boy's family came to view our daughter;" "bride viewing," "we showed the girl to the boy," "the boy came to look at her," "I interviewed her," "we interviewed each other" "they brought this proposal," "is the marriage settled ?", "they match each other perfectly," "they showed me lot of girls... then I agreed to marry her"...

Men and women of this study also refer to their first meeting as an "interview" and men more often than women say, *"when I interviewed her"* or women say, *"when he interviewed me,"* suggesting a calculated rational approach to marriage and gender power imbalance. While educated women have their freedom to choose the man they want to marry and turn down a proposal their parents have made, ultimately it is the man and his family who call the shots !

It is a commonly held opinion that men marry women for their physical attractiveness and women marry men for their ability to provide, as well as for their status, professional or financial driving ambition. In an extensive cross-cultural study by Buss *et al.*, (1990), a gender differential is noted; women consistently seek men with earning potential and men seek women with youth and beauty. As some socio-biologists argue, it is to a woman's advantage to seek an economically resourceful man who can help support her offspring, whereas men seek young attractive women for the genetic advantage of producing healthy offspring. Pines (1999) argues that women have a greater parental investment, meaning energy and time invested in raising an offspring than men; hence women show caution in choosing men with substantial earning potentials, so that her offspring survives.

In this study, an overwhelming majority of the female respondents decided to marry their husbands **mainly** because of the men's economic resources and capability, educational qualifications and family background, and appealing personality traits. As in Puri's (1999) study on middle and upper class women, for women of this study, desirable qualities of a husband are: *"understanding husband," "a considerate husband" "not exploitative"* and *"a caring husband."* Nevertheless, women respondents emphasized that the economic capability and educational qualifications of men are more important than their physical attractiveness and other unimportant qualities. Even if they wished to marry *"tall, handsome, dark men with a good physique"* they compromised on them for good income and professional qualifications:

"I had fantasized about marrying a tall, handsome man... but my husband is short, average looking... but in other aspects he is more than what I had imagined... educationally, intellectually and sexually."

Women are expected to compromise on men's inadequacies or negative points, and adjust to men's requirements more than vice versa. Parents and other older relatives point out that, *"he might not be good looking, he might be short, dark, balding, but he will take good care of you."*

Both the parents and the future bride have discriminating taste about a potential suitor's economic resources. Male's resources are considered more valuable than females, thus resulting in inequality, domination, double standard, and a more subservient position for women. But even when educational qualification of a woman is higher than the man, more importance is given to a man, while recognizing the educational accomplishment of a woman: a female physician married a man from the U.S.A. with a master's degree in computer engineering. Their relatives commented about the "*good match,*" but added, "*she is lucky to have him!*"

In keeping with the cultural norm that a male should have higher status than a female, a marriage gradient exists– men tend to marry down, (hypogamy) that is, they marry women who have lower educational, economic and occupational status than them and are younger in age. Women marry up, (a cultural practice known as hypergamy) – they marry men who have more economic resources, education, status, influence and power than them. This not only improves a woman's economic status, but the status of her parents, also. Nevertheless, there are marriages between partners who have similar professions, educational and economic status.

The majority of male respondents decided to marry their wives mainly because of their "*physical attraction,*" "*fair skin,*" "*education,*" "*domestic capabilities,*" "*family background,*" "*good character,*" *and* "*good nature.*" These were the frequently mentioned attributes that acted as decisive factors. It is not surprising that in a marriage negotiation, a man's sexual past is ignored, but enormous importance is given to the "*good character*" of the potential bride, thus creating a double standard. Hindus consider virginity as a state of *dharma*, a symbol of respectability, family honor and a valued resource in a marriage settlement. In fact, there is a part in the Hindu marriage ritual, where the bride's father gives her as a personal gift to her husband, called *kanydhana*– the "gift of a virgin". This ritual is supposed to absolve a father of his sins. Virginity is also meant to preserve caste purity, hence premarital female sexuality is socially controlled. Women are also expected to preserve the blood purity of their husbands' lineage and any indiscreet sexual behavior may jeopardize this, her status and violate the expectations of her husband's family.

A young woman without a good reputation and questionable moral character is squeezed out of the marriage market. Marriage matchmakers do a good background check on the character of the future bride, indirectly asking people about her character. Arranged marriage assures men of virginity of women. A male bank official says, *"It was important that I should marry a virgin and she was... everybody expects that... that is why many of my friends went for an arranged marriage...because we are sure of this (virginity)."*

A male professor of Sanskrit, a subject of this study, explained the reason for men's preference for arranged marriage. *"In love marriage (romantic marriages), people suspect the girl's character, but they don't suspect or condemn man's premarital or extramarital relationships... after all Lord Krishna had lots of lovers!"*

Indian society's norms regarding virginity for women before marriage facilitates men in gaining power over women and control over their resources. The same standards of virginity (purity) do not necessarily apply to men- even when parents know about their sons' premarital relationships, it is quite often ignored or de-emphasized, or the issue is diffused. After all men need to "release their body tension," or "they have to gain experience," they say.

As Foucault (1978) argues, societies control sexuality by establishing differential norms for appropriate male and female sexual behavior. In Indian society, a man's loss of virginity gives him experience and enhances his masculinity, but the same act devalues women and diminishes her "lady" status to a "loose woman" or an "impure woman."

Men in this study also stressed attributes such as, *"good mother," "good housewife," "should not be argumentative," "an understanding wife," "should take good care of my parents."* More men than women give importance to physical attractiveness. Interestingly, many of the western criteria of an ideal husband or a wife such as, "sense of humor," "interesting," "fun to be with," "sexy," "exciting," "romantic," "friendly," "cultured," "interest in sports and travels," "he should not have feelings of insecurity" were not mentioned.

Horoscope compatibilities of the suitable partners also played a key role in their decision to marry. Orthodox, but educated, urban Hindus consult astrologers before finalizing marriage plans of their children. The astrologers predict the future of marriage and compatibility of marital partners, based on relative positions of the planets and stars at a particular time.

After everything is said and done, if the astrologers do not approve of a marriage, the wedding plans collapse. The astrologers are astute key players in the marriage game–they can make or break a marriage plan. They can align and realign the stars and planets according to the consultation fees !

It may be appropriate to see arranged marriage and sexual practices from the perspective of **SCRIPTING THEORY** as developed by Laumann and Gagnon (1995). Sexuality is a social construction–the sexual customs, practices, values and expectations orchestrated by culture have a powerful impact on individuals. The processes of socialization, acculturation and social interactions are likely to influence individuals' sexual conduct. Another social constructionist, Plummer (1984), states that sexual norms are culture specific and each culture defines "who restrictions" and "how restrictions;" some of the factors related to "who restrictions" are gender of the partner, age, race, caste, and class. (cited in Weeks 2003:21).

The authors also stress the importance of "master status" and its characteristics in relation to sexual conduct. People are likely to have sexual relationships with people who have a similar master status to their own and similar economic status to their own. This is quite evident in Indian arranged marriages; one's caste, class and religious affiliation contribute to his/her master status that direct individuals to choose their marriage partners within the group who have a similar master status. Marriages and sexual behavior in India are strongly directed by cultural script; the caste culture insists on the endogamous nature of marriage and sexual relationships.

The following segment on Hinduism's perspective on sex, and sexual beliefs and practices of the interviewees of this study (which will be discussed later on) further reinforces Laumann and Gagnon's view that scripts for sexual conduct are derived from culture. Sex is a social construct. In Weeks (2003:19) discussion of human sexuality, sex and society are seen as inseparable domains with variability of sexual forms, beliefs, ideologies and sexual cultures. Hinduism seems to play a significant role in shaping the values, beliefs and practices regarding sex. As Schwartz and Rutter argue that a society's norms, transmitted through social structures and everyday life are so powerful, "that it is impossible to imagine the absence of norms that control sexuality" (1998:18).

SEX–A CENTRAL ASPECT OF HINDUISM

In order to understand the sexual behaviors and attitudes of subjects of this study and how they adjust to each other sexually, it is necessary to explain the Hinduism perspective on sex. Hinduism may not be the only source of their sexual socialization. Watching pornography movies; reading sex manuals, magazines, books; and information on the specifics of sexual acts transmitted from sexually experienced relatives and friends to the inexperienced ones contribute to the sexual awareness of people as stated later. Nevertheless, Hinduism's approach to sex influences people's attitudes towards sex. Indian ancient literatures and myths reveal an openness of human sexuality; creation is a joyous act of intercourse and gods and goddesses are shown in ecstatic embrace. Hinduism has sacramental views on sex; it remains a central and a natural aspect of human beings. Such is the acceptance of sex that an excerpt from the Vedic literature says: "Human life is based on sex... *Kama* (love or sex) is the thread that runs through the garland, but never seen." (trans. by Sathyam). Danielou (1994:43) in his translation of the *Kamasutra* by Vatsayana states the importance of sex -- "Sexuality is essential for the survival of man, just as food is necessary for bodily health and on them depend both virtue (*dharma*) and wealth (*artha*)." As noted earlier, Hinduism regards *kama* (pleasures of sex or the life of senses) as one of the three aims of marriage. In *Mahabharatha*, quoted by Meyer (1930:331) states "without *kama* a man has no wish for worldly profit, without *kama* a man does not strive after the good (dharma), without *kama*, a man does not love, therefore *kama* stands above the others."

"*Kama* is the innermost core (of the world)... in it is founded *dharma* and *artha* ... without *Kama* the manifold workings of the dharma would not be thinkable." In the *Upanishads*, it is stated that there is no joy in anything as much as there is in *kama*. Also in *Ramayana*, as cited by Meyer "sexual union is the law and the right of the body" (1995:332)

K.M. Panikkar in introducing Kamasutra, edited by W.G. Archer (1963) states that Hindu holy scriptures such as the *Rig Veda, Mahabharatha, Ramayana, Atharvaveda, Gita Govinda, and the Upanishads* deal with love and sex in an explicit, positive manner. Some of these literature support the view that spiritual union with God, mukthi (redemption or salvation) and improvement in *karma* (one's fate) could be attained by sexual union. The supreme bliss that is attained by ritual sexuality is compared to the bliss of divine experience. Sexual union between male and female is considered a religious duty, sacred and sacramental, exalting it to the level of the union of gods-- *Shiva and Shakthi* who created the universe through their union. It is this adoration of sexual union of gods that explains the reason for worshipping *Shiva* in the symbol of *lingam* (phallic symbol) and worshipping *Shakthi* in the symbol of *yoni* (vagina). *Yoni* is also considered as a sacred area, a symbol of cosmic mysteries, the sacred mouth of the creator. *Tantric* philosophy explicitly describes human sexuality; *kundalini*, the serpentine power of enlightenment and sexual enjoyment is said to lie in a coiled up state in the perineum, that is, between the anus and the phallus/vagina of the human body. Through skillful sexual techniques and yoga, the serpentine power can be awakened and shoot up the spine into the cerebrum of the brain.

Gita Govinda, the twelth century erotic poem that is treasured by millions of Hindus, depicts the love story of Lord Krishna and his married lover Radha. Radha's sexual passion for Krishna symbolizes the soul's intense longing for God and God's intense love for the soul. Gita Govinda describes the divine-human love making in sensual terms. It reads, they achieved ecstatic bliss in love-making, Radha "lying over his beautiful body, to triumph over her lover," until "her thighs grew lifeless' and her eyes became heavy and closed" (Parrinder,

1980:31 from Gita Govinda, tran by G. Keyt, 1947) In Hinduism gods themselves engage in sexual activities, posing as role models to humans in their uninhibited and ultimate enjoyment of sex.

Hindu rituals of sexual union can be traced back to the Vedas. Sexual intercourse is treated as a sacred religious ritual beginning with personal physical purification, prayers, sacrifices and other rituals. Conception is still viewed as sacred, sometimes invoking gods through prayer and rituals. In the ritual wedding bath, a Brahminic priest asks the bridegroom to repeat the following *mantra* (prayer) from the *Vedas*:

"Oh Kama, it is you who gives me power for sex... bring her to me... she is just like wine for me... I prepare myself for her by applying honey" (in the traditional ritual bath, honey is applied to the private parts of bride and the groom to intensify their sexual desire).

In another wedding ritual, the bridegroom is asked to repeat this *mantra* to his bride from *Paraskara griha sutra ; "take me to the highest happiness... open your thighs... don't oblige me... you desire it and open it... with equal desire... we shall... all our desires are based on this..."*

(translation provided by vedic scholar Satyam, who said the mantras are chanted by the priests in Sanskrit without giving translation to the couple or the guests)

Many Hindu oral traditions, folklore, proverbs and songs reflect the celebration of the uninhibited joys of sex. Raheja and Gold's examination of Rajasthani folk culture represented in the form of songs and stories, often performed in the weddings and festivals reveal explicit description of sexual engagement, raw sexuality, sensuality and promiscuity. The language that is used in these erotic songs and stories is vulgar, but yet socially acceptable: "If you want to fuck, go up on the hill... Lover"... from there you can see Delhi and Agra"; "your penis is a pipal tree's trunk" (1994:40,63).

Traditional Hinduism's view on human sexuality at times is one of contradiction. Although considerable importance is given to kama, as one of the three aims of life, Hindu religious scriptures also treat sexual abstinence as a virtue. Hindu literature promotes the joys of sex, but at the same time encourages sexual intercourse only during a period of time when a woman is in her *ritu*, that is, from the fourth day after her menstruation, considered a propitious time for conception. Not approaching one's wife sexually during her ritu is considered a sin, violation of the husband's duty and the wife's sexual rights.

Meyer (1995:218) quotes *Ramayana*, which states *"cohabitation in the ritu is one of the virtues leading to heaven." "Sexual union is the law and right of the body"* (332). On the other hand, Hindu holy scriptures prohibit sexual intercourse between husband and wife during "inauspicious" times; full-moon days, new moon and half-moon days and also during certain festival days, because of the fear of unhealthy conception. Sexual intercourse with wives during menstruation time is seen as a defilement of husbands. Furthermore, the importance Hinduism gives to procreation as the main reason for sexual union is likely to lessen the enjoyment of sex for recreational purpose.

It is a common belief among Hindus that semen is a very valued resource and has to be used sparingly for "it takes forty days, and forty drops of blood to make one drop of semen." Some Hindus are convinced that men can achieve a higher salvation by practicing coitus *reservatus*. Withholding ejaculation stores the semen in the head, the epicenter of human divinity, thus enhancing males divinity.

Kulhara and Avasthi (1995), Kakar (1989), and Moni Nag (1996) in their analysis of sexual dysfunctions among Indian males have commented that this exaltation of semen has resulted in anxiety, neurosis, sexual dilemmas and lack of sexual enjoyment among some men. Kulhara and Avasthi's findings from research on male sexual dysfunction indicate that sexual dysfunction problems of males are linked to a uniquely culturally related neurosis called *"Dhat syndrome"*. Men with *"dhat syndrome"* complain of symptoms of fatigue, listlessness and loss of appetite. They also complain about sexual dysfunction and anxieties about sexual performance. These symptoms are attributed, by men with dhat syndrome, to excess of sexual activity and masturbation that drains them of their precious dhat (semen). Loss of semen is considered detrimental to their health. Kulhara and Avasthi state that the presence of this cultural myth, the "dhat syndrome" – a preoccupation and guilt associated with loss of "valuable" semen is likely to cause psycho-sexual dysfunction, erectile dysfunction and sexual performance anxieties.

Hinduism's ambivalent attitude towards sex is also seen in its treatment of sexual abstinence as a virtue after the Grihasta (householder) stage. "Realization of self" could be attained by practicing asceticism through sexual abstinence or transforming sexual energy into spirituality. Kakar's (1989) discussion of Indian sexuality also indicates cultural injunctions such as ritu and avoidance of sex on certain "inauspicious" days fearing unhealthy conception and other sexual misconceptions aggravate marital strain due to sexual dissatisfaction and act as an impediment to a fully satisfied sex life.

HINDUISM'S PERSPECTIVE ON WOMEN AND THEIR SEXUALITY

A general understanding of Hinduism's views on women is necessary for the discussion of the sexual attitudes and acts, and for the marital relationships of men and women of this study.

Hinduism views woman with contradictions; she is elevated to the pedestal, treated with respect and as a great source of pleasure, but also treated as a subordinate and inferior. As stated earlier, it is a Hindu belief that a woman can achieve purification of body, soul and salvation through marriage. She takes part in only one *sanskara* (ritual) in her life, that is the marriage ritual, unlike a man who does sixteen *sanskaras* in his life. She gains atonement and reconciliation only through her son, suggesting her devaluation without bearing a son.

On the other hand, Meyer (1995:495) comments that in no other literature other than Hindu epics is there such heartfelt appreciation of women. He quotes from the epics which states, "Honor women... for of a truth it is from women the good (*dharma*), and all the pleasures of love come."

Danielou, quoting from the Vedic literature which stresses the importance of woman, states "Being the source of virtue, woman is the best means of reaching heaven ..." (1994:25). A wife is seen as a husband's *dharmapatni* (dutiful wife or helpmate in the performance of religious ritual); without his wife beside her, a husband is not allowed to perform *poojas* (prayers or fire sacrifices to gods). A woman who achieves wifehood is in a "state of personal as well as collective *dharma*: being well placed in the context of such norms means being properly related to oneself and the society at large" states Khare (1982:154).

A woman's importance and her value are mainly attached to her relational role with her husband and procreating children, particularly begetting a son. This is her raison d'etre. Mitter points out, "The ability to give birth, and sustain life, to conceive sons and assure the continuity of the lineage, is woman's supreme virtue" (1991:89). A woman is made to feel as though her identity is of less importance, but can achieve the same through her husband. It is the marital and maternal role that gives her status and recognition. But according to the Vedas, men too have similar expectations: *"He alone is a perfect man who consists of his wife, himself and his offspring. A man who does not win a wife is really half and he is not a full man as long as he does not beget an offspring"* (cited by Basu, 2001:22).

The importance given to maternal role is also noted by Gough (1993:167), who suggests mother is highly valued, because of her procreative power to perpetuate the patrilineal line and also wife is considered as the embodiment of the procreative strength of her husband, based on the mythological belief of the ideal couple *Shiva* and *Parvathi*. Khare (1982:157) citing Manu indicates how Manu exaggerates the status of mother, characterizing her as the earth, as "presiding over the earth" (Manu IV:183). According to Kane (1941:580-581), in *Dharmasastra*, a mother has a highly exalted status and a son may prefer her over his father because she "bore him."

Meyer (1995:199) citing *Mahabharatha*, writes, mother is elevated to a position higher than guru;

"of all guru the mother is the highest guru... no guru to equal the mother." Without these relational roles of wife and mother she is a persona non grata. Pychoanalyzing feminine identity, Kakar (1981:56) argues, "her identity is wholly defined by her relationship to others... an Indian woman knows that motherhood confers upon her a purpose and identity that nothing else in her culture can. Each infant borne and nurtured by her safely into childhood, especially if the child is a son, is both certification and redemption."

The Atharva Veda sees woman as a pleasure giver and procreator of sons. It says,

"Wife stretch yourself with pleasure on the bed and procreate sons for your husband... You will be blessed like the queen of heaven." In another quote, man prays to God to protect his woman and *"inspire her so that she realizes my wish, full of desire as I am, and that opening her thighs, she allows my penis to assail her vagina"* (Danielou, 1994:30) In the Hindu view, as discussed by Vatsayana in Kama Sutra, a woman has a much stronger erotic disposition and her delight in the sexual act is much greater than a man's. Mitter (1991:87) points out the sexual insatiability and lust of women as represented in *Mahabharata*. She cites,

The fire has never too many logs,
the ocean never too many rivers,
death never too many souls,
and fair-eyed woman never too many men.

But yet she is expected to be sexually submissive; in the Hindu wedding ritual as the bridegroom holds the bride's right hand and walks around the holy fire, he repeats after the priest, "be submissive in all love acts and give me your love to our full satisfaction" (Sathyam 1997:12). But an universal Hindu cultural icon, *Lingha* which represents the symbol of the Lord Shiva, depicts him in sexual union with his consort *Parvathi*, suggesting the indispensable nature of the female sexual power-*shakti* for creation. In Hindu mythology, *Shakti* as a manifestation of *Parvathi* has power, energy, strength and other male-like qualities.

Women are also seen as the preservers of caste purity, as well as the purity of their husbands' lineage. Harlan and Courtright argue that the "responsibility for maintaining the blood purity of the husband's line falls heavily upon the wife." A wife/woman is expected to conduct her actions in a honorable manner, preserve her chastity and perform rituals that will maintain her household purity and the well-being of her husband (1995:6). Furthermore, social control on unmarried females' sexuality is emphasized by considering "virginity as a state of dharma"– the right moral conduct (Khare: 1982:152). Female virginity is an invaluable asset in the marriage market and a prerequisite for marriage settlement (Srinivas 1984, Kakar 1981, Derné 1994). Puri, discussing the societal expectations of female sexuality states that her female subjects give great importance to premarital virginity and chastity in "keeping with the a national cultural tradition" (1999:111).

Generally speaking, Indian women are seen as a repository of Hindu values. Hinduism has laid down rather rigid expectations of a wife that results in the subordination of her welfare, interests, and desires to her husband's welfare; for such a woman is called *pathivratha*, a devoted wife and the ultimate ideal woman. It is said that as a river merges into an ocean and loses its identity, so a wife is supposed to merge with her husband and lose her identity. Kakar (1978:66) argues that there is a "formidable consensus" in Indian society promoting *Sita* as the ideal exemplary woman; "the ideal of womanhood incorporated by *Sita* is one of chastity, purity, gentle tenderness and singular faithfulness." Although there may be different interpretations of the portrayal of women in the great epics *Mahabahratha* and *Ramayana*, the epics extol women such as *Sita, Shakuntala, Savitri* and *Damayanthi, Draupadi* who are virtuous, devoted, uncomplaining, long-suffering and self-sacrificing and the very embodiment of *pathivratha*. In admiring *Shakuntala*, it is said, *"she is a wife whose life is her husband, she is a wife who keeps holy loyalty to her husband."*

An excerpt from the *Mahabharatha* says, *"even when the husband crosses over into another birth, when he dies... the faithful mate follows ever after him." " she the steadfast in virtue, who eats not before I have eaten... stands not unless I stand... lies to rest only when I lie"* (Meyer: 1995; 340-343).

Contradictory expectations are seen in the societal attitudes of women, based on the opposing qualities of Hindu goddess; women are expected to be powerful and submissive, strong and gentle, courageous and timid, virtuous and virtueless. Since female goddesses are worshipped with the same fervor as male gods, devaluation of female goddess is not indicated. They are seen as both creators and destroyers. Goddess *Kali*, is depicted with garland of skulls around her neck, her tongue dripping with blood; she demonstrates raging anger, danger, and the obliterating power. Whereas, goddess *Parvathi, Sita, Saraswathi* represent ultimate female beauty, gentleness, passivity and maternal warmth. There is this belief that women are capable of acting like destructive *Kali*, hence their behavior should be controlled and molded like Parvathi or Sita; "for society to prosper, women's power must be channeled toward procreation and the protection of the family" (Harlan and Courtright (1995:11).

Menon and Shweder (1994:73) point out an additional aspect of the goddess Kali–also seen as the Great mother goddess in Orissa. Their male and female narratives see "the ultimate message of the icon *Kali* is to display the cultural "truth" that it is women who uphold the social order... (they) are the centrifuges that hold the families together." Interestingly their subjects do not attribute too much importance to males as they "contribute only financially to the welfare of the family" (1994:73). Noting the ambiguous nature and the contradictory societal expectations of Indian women, Mitter notes, "nothing in the Hindu culture prevents a forceful woman" from reaching a powerful position, but "at the same time, ordinary women, whatever their portion of goddess like power, must be subordinated and constrained" (1991:80).

Kakar (1990:17) too points out another dichotomous nature of Indian women; the Hindu mythology, Indian movies and folklore reveal an "age-old yet still persisting cultural splitting of the wife into a mother and a whore." He states that "as a female sexual being... the patriarchal culture's horror and scorn are heaped upon the hapless wife." Thus, Indian society expects women to have purity and ultimate goodness of great goddess, but their expression of sexuality and sensuality may not be socially acceptable as they challenge the society's image of women.

Indian women's image is rather complex, complicated and ambiguous at times. As Seymour (1999:272) puts it aptly from Western point of view, "... what Westerners often misconstrue as passivity in Indian women is deferential behavior appropriate to some circumstances that can be transformed into assertive and dominant behavior in other circumstances." Women of this study are university educated professionals, but yet in their interactions with their husbands and children, actions within the family, and in their views on arranged marriage, they seem to have a strategy of **reconciliation without renunciation** regarding traditional expectations of women. In their professional and family roles, they display power, importance, authority and respect--sociocultural expectations associated with their roles.

A personal note should be added here about the societal expectations of professional women. As a woman socialized in an urban, university educated professional family, I was expected to be the "total woman" – highly educated, good professional, good wife, good mother, good homemaker; deferential, caring, warm and hospitable woman to the extended family and to friends. An admirable woman is one who can balance all these roles skillfully without complaining and compromising on the expectations of any role, while retaining the "traditional" nature of females. Mothers may not frequently refer to the epic women such as *Sita, Savitri* as role models in socializing girls, but even occasional reference to them influences girls developing the concept of an ideal woman. In addition, educational and professional aspiration of girls are stoked by using professional aunts and female cousins and extraordinary world famous females as the reference group. Gender differences in socialization is taken for granted. Although there is subtle operation of son preference even among middle and upper classes, girls are encouraged to succeed educationally and professionally. Societal expectations of a woman are rather high, multifaceted, unrealistic and stressful at times; they could be more demanding than they are for males.

2

IS THERE ANY LOVE OR SEXUAL ATTRACTION BEFORE THE MARRIAGE ?

Generally speaking, it is a stereotypical assumption that in Western societies romantic involvement with a particular person mainly determines one's decision to marry that person. But in Indian society, primarily the decision to marry determines the choice of a marital partner. Since arranged marriage is not entirely based on romantic love or sexual attraction, it is interesting to find out whether, when, and how love and sexual attraction develops between marriage partners. After the marriage negotiators and prospective marriage partners are satisfied with the personal resources of eligible mates, a visitation or meeting or "interview" is arranged at one of their homes to physically evaluate each other and observe their personality characteristics.

If at this point they happen to like each other, a marriage alliance is finalized with the approval of prospective mates, their parents and extended family. Generally, there is a formal engagement or an informal engagement with a firm understanding that the young couple has agreed to marry each other. It is intended that the engagement period will give a chance for the engaged couple to get acquainted with each other and also it gives adequate time for marriage preparation. An engagement period of more than six months is not usually recommended for fear of a man changing his mind or some unpredictable incident that may disrupt the marriage plans.

It is relevant to note here, in this study, approximately 50% of the total sample had an acquaintance of four months with each other before they married, 27% had an acquaintance with each other for six months to one year and 17% had met each other only two times before the wedding day. During this acquaintance period, the individuals met each other in their homes, or went for movies, restaurants or for walks in the park or attended family functions together. A very small number of them had known each other for several years or since childhood as they were their relatives.

The majority of the total sample, that is, 52% of the sample, reported that they did **not** have any mutual sexual attraction and any presence of feelings of love when they met each other the **first** few times. But 49% of the total sample developed mutual sexual attraction and love during their period of acquaintance. In fact, 24% of the total sample felt instant sexual attraction towards their mates when they met each other for the very first time. It is also interesting to note that nearly 46% of them developed mutual sexual attraction and love only **after** the marriage and .05% had no sexual attraction towards their mates either before or even after several years of marriage.

The respondents of this study are divided into **three** groups:

1. LOVE AND SEXUAL ATTRACTION BEFORE THE MARRIAGE GROUP

2. LOVE AND SEXUAL ATTRACTION AFTER THE MARRIAGE GROUP

3. A very small group (1% of the total sample) of people who developed love during their engagement period, but did not develop sexual attraction or physical intimacy before the marriage.

(It should be noted here the first category of people is referred to as the Love and Sexual Attraction Before the Marriage because they had feelings of love and sexual attraction before they got married; whereas, the second group developed love and sexual attraction after the marriage. For the sake of brevity, they are referred to as **"The Before-Marriage Group" and "The After-Marriage Group".**)

The Before-Marriage Group refers to the 49% of the total sample who developed love and sexual attraction during their period of acquaintance or engagement before the marriage. In this Before group, males constitute a higher percentage than females. That is, males make up 58% of the group, but females make up 41% of the group.

It is important to remember that even for this group, it was not sexual attraction or romantic love that determined their decision to marry, rather it was the similar caste and class; and educational and professional compatibility that determined their decision to marry. *"Sex was not the foremost thing... it was at the back of my mind... given time and place, I knew it will develop"* says a male charted accountant.

A small percentage of the sample felt sexually attracted to their mate when they met each other for the very first time. The majority of the respondents who belong to this group, "dated" or had romantic love within the context of arranged marriage. They went to restaurants, movies, parks, exchanged letters and gifts, and spent hours on the phone. They also had physical intimacy such as holding hands, kissing, fondling and caressing. A small number of them said they "*did everything*" except having sexual intercourse. The functionality of arranged marriage does not necessarily exclude the possibility of romance and passion; in fact it lights the fire of passion among alike partners. It is a misconception to think arranged marriage kills romance.

Just three people "reported" that they had premarital sex with their future mates during the period of acquaintance. A small number of them did not go out with their fiancées or their future spouses for fear of societal disapproval, but they spent time with each other in the presence of their parents.

Several possible conclusions may be made from the interviews with the **Before-Marriage Group.**

ROMANTIC LOVE AND SEXUAL ATTRACTION

The Before-Marriage Group developed romantic love and sexual attraction during the period of engagement as in the case of romantic marriages. They felt that engagement was crucial as it gave them a chance to get to know each other and communicate with each other. More than anything, the engagement period helped them to develop sexual attraction and love. Both men and women had many thoughts about it:

"We had romance during the six months of engagement... it helped us to get sexually attracted to each other and develop love" says an engineer.

"We had passionate feelings for each other during the engagement period" comments a female English professor.

"We were sexually attracted to each other and began to love each other... we had a fantastic period of romance."

"The very first day I fell in love with her...touched her... kissed her in the open field at 7 p.m... Except sexual intercourse, we did everything during the engagement period" says a program executive.

One businesswoman comments, *"We were sexually attracted as soon as we met... Two hours after we met, we decided to marry. We did everything except sexual intercourse."*

Although premarital sex is not uncommon among contemporary educated young urbanites, the majority of the men and women of this study did not want to have premarital sex with their fiancées. This again confirms the argument of the social construction of sexuality, that sexuality is shaped by social forces. Although Hinduism is a pro-sex religion, yet the society considers sex before or outside the marriage disruptive and dangerous. A few men in this study that felt they were ready to have premarital sex, but their fiancées resisted the idea or they had cultural constrictions. They commented:

"I would have loved to make love to her, but she didn't want it";

"If the societal restrictions were not there, I would have liked to have premarital sex," says a professor of biology.

"I kissed her, held her hands, fondled her breasts... but that is where it had to be stopped... !" says a program executive.

"I didn't want to have premarital sex. Because our minds are conditioned like that... I was not prepared... We are bound to traditions. We have respect for the sanctity of marriage," says a female college professor.

"If she had asked for it I would have been put off with her. If I would have had premarital sex, I would have gone down in my own self-esteem and she would have gone down in her self-esteem and my esteem of her" comments an engineer.

Indian society is a shame oriented society and family honor is zealously guarded. Societal disapproval of premarital sex and unwanted pregnancy before marriage and the stigma attached to such an act discourages individuals from consummating their relationship before the wedding. Indian society is more concerned about *"what will people say,"* than individuals' own happiness, pleasure, comfort and convenience. *"I just touched her, but couldn't kiss her and do the other things... it is indecent doing it in the public, what will they think !"*, says a university professor. Furthermore, Indian society is a highly ritualistic society. There are rituals for all significant events in one's life, even for when a child makes a transition from only milk food to solid food. The ritual is called "the first rice ritual." So, the idea of consummating one's relationship without a Hindu ritual is not desirable. Also there is fear that conception without the rituals may lead to deformed babies.

Mothers often stress the importance of the preservation of virginity until marriage and warn their daughters against losing it as they would be considered as "damaged goods" or "character not good" in the marriage market. *"Once men get sexually excited it is difficult to stop them... so don't excite them"* is a warning given by some mothers to their daughters. Glorification of virginity or norms regarding premarital chastity, the sanctity of marriage, and the fear of consummating a relationship without the prescribed religious ritual -- all discourage individuals from consummating their relationship before marriage. But, then there is the fear that a man may change his mind about the marriage or lose interest in a woman if he becomes sexually familiar with her before marriage. Mothers and older women keep a watchful eye on engaged women and warn them not to "demystify" the sexual act and lose their sexual respectability. One woman's comments seem to sum up the beliefs of women in general, *"We are brought up in such a way that we believe we should be virgins on the wedding night."*

What the respondents' attitudes towards premarital sex suggest is that individuals conduct their sexual behavior according to the directions of cultural scripts and their social networks, meaning parents, relatives, and friends also determine their decisions related to sex. Puri (1999) in her analysis of Indian middle and upper-middle class women's sexuality and desire, notes the role of mothers in disciplining, regulating and controlling the bodies and sexual lives of their daughters. She argues that social/sexual restrictions act as a "direct grip" on women's bodies and desire.

Other interesting reasons were revealed for not having premarital sex during the engagement period. They are, to build anticipation for sex on the First Night and to remember and cherish that night as the most memorable and significant day in their lives. Women commented;

" I wanted to build anticipation for the first night"; " I wanted to keep it for the wedding night". It is also these ideas; that couples should get to know each other before they have sex and sex is an inevitable reality of marriage that one need not hurry to have it, help them to postpone sex until marriage.

Even men are sexually temperate and expressed their attitude of deferred gratification and self-discipline towards premarital sex. A male radio and T.V. engineer comments,

"anyway it (sex) is there after marriage... my conscience didn't permit me to have premarital sex. I told my wife we can wait to have sex even after marriage... we have a long life. First, let us have a good understanding of each other".

"I had deferred gratification about premarital sex... I thought anyway it is going to happen, let it happen in its own time... I kept that for a special

day". (a male professor of Botany)

THE AFTER-MARRIAGE GROUP:

As stated earlier the majority of the sample did not have any sexual attraction or feelings of love towards their prospective mates on their first encounters. Approximately 46% of the sample developed love and sexual attraction gradually and slowly after the marriage. The males make up 37% of the After Marriage Group, whereas females make up 63% of the same.

What do men and women respondents of this group say about sexual attraction?

Women say, *"There was no sexual attraction at the beginning...it was not the main criteria... understanding each other was important."*

"I didn't have any sexual attraction or urge towards him" or *"I never looked at him with sexual interest when I met him."*

"Absolutely no sexual attraction when I met him... I took a risk."

"We were not thinking about sexual attraction... I just wanted to know him, his thinking, his views, whether I can adjust myself to his family..."

"Sexual attraction was secondary."

"I didn't even think about sexual attraction... I am the eldest daughter to my parents... so I had to marry."

Men said, *"There was not much sexual attraction... I liked her... I was looking for a long-time marital relationship, not immediate sexual attraction."*

"Sexual attraction was not the most important thing."

What should be noted here is that the males are more likely to be in the Before-Marriage Group, and females are more likely to be in the After-Marriage Group. Perhaps, this could be again explained by socio-biological theory; men are looking for youth and beauty and women are looking for economic resources.

The majority of this group reported that they took up to six months, while a small number of them took one year to develop feelings of love and sexual attraction. And also, as the interviews with women reveal, they take a longer time than their husbands to develop sexual attraction and interest in their husbands.

Although there was an absence of any sexual attraction and love, individuals who belong to this group decided to marry their mates because of their similarities, compatible characteristics, valued personal resources and matching of the horoscopes. This group seems to de-emphasize the importance of sexual attraction and love for a marriage, rather they give considerable importance to education, professional qualities and economic capability. A good character, understanding nature, family background, responsibility to extended family members and domestic capabilities also occupy high priority for them. These are evident in these statements of both men and women:

"I had very little sexual attraction, but I liked him... I agreed to marry him because of his good education and good family... after one year of marriage, I began to love him" "there was no sexual attraction at the beginning... we were attracted to each other by our ideas... both of us like music... it took one year after the marriage to love him."

"I never looked at him with sexual interest...I married him because of all the compatibility I had with him."

"Sexual attraction was not there for her... later on after the marriage, it developed... I didn't pay too much attention to it before I got married because other factors were compatible."

Unlike the Before-Marriage Group, the After-Marriage Group did not have physical intimacy during the period of engagement, obviously for the reason they were not sexually attracted to each other or had developed emotional intimacy with each other. This group insisted that physical intimacy was not important, rather *"it is more important to get to know each other."*

Considerable importance is given to starting a married life--fulfilling the obligations of the life stage *grihastha* (householder) and to fulfill *dharma* towards one's parents by getting married. Whether the person one intends to marry has the financial, caring and adjustment capability to care for the elderly parents are more important than love and sexual attraction before marriage. The comment "I was more interested in starting my married life than in sexual attraction" seems to sum up the essence of the After-Marriage Group.

Love and sexual attraction are considered by this group as a consequence of marriage and not a prerequisite for marriage:

"I wanted a marriage partner; I didn't look for sexual attraction... I don't think not having sexual attraction has any effect on marriage... after marriage we got close and then sexual attraction developed" comments a female teacher.

"Sexual attraction is not necessary before the marriage once you start living with a person, it comes naturally," reports a female manager.

These comments suggest marriage paves the way for love and mutual sexual fondness and once a newly married couple gets accustomed to each other, eventually these feelings emerge. Unlike romantic love marriages where love, sexual attraction, compatibilities and desire to be together determine the decision to marry, arranged marriage system determines the person one should marry based on similarities. Living together on a daily basis leads to the development of conjugal love gradually. The process of development of love will be discussed later on.

ARE FEELINGS OF LOVE AND SEXUAL ATTRACTION SPONTANEOUS OR CULTIVATED AND CONDITIONED?

It is no mystery as to how you can develop sexual attraction and love towards a stranger that has been arranged to meet you by your parents and extended family. It appears love and sexual attraction are cultivated, concocted and developed gradually when two young and healthy people with similar backgrounds are brought together. Do love and sexual attraction develop "in vitro" ? The arranged marriage system creates conducive conditions for the cultivation of sexual attraction and love with an individual that has the compatible qualities necessary for a good marriage. Cultural conditioning and socialization shape the minds of individuals to accept a compatible person as their marriage partner and then the individuals **learn** to like the person sexually and emotionally. *"I am marrying, therefore I must learn to love and have sexual attraction"* is a unique rationalization described as this;

"Intentionally I loved him because I was going to marry him... I was going to marry him so I must love him." (a female government official)

"You have everything going for you... he is very eligible... What do you want ?... you make yourself fall in love with him." (a female assistant professor)

"If you don't get what you like, you have to like what you get" (a male bank official)

"We are brought up in such a way to think that you get married... eventually you get used to him sexually... it is assumed that sexual attraction and compatibility will develop somehow" (a college educated housewife)

The decision to marry someone compatible and similar, per se, instills in people emotional intimacy and physical attraction:

"We developed sexual attraction because we were getting married... I began to love him." (a female physician)

"Sexual attraction towards her began when I came to know that I was marrying her." (a male professor)

"I would have been sexually attracted to her anyway because of the four months of courtship after our engagement. When we see a girl whom we are going to marry, mentally we begin to imagine her face, figure... mentally we are prepared during courtship to develop sexual attraction." (a male bank officer)

The development of love and sexual attraction in both the Before Marriage Group and After Marriage Group suggests that if two people with striking socio-cultural similarities marry and if there is compatibility-- these will lead eventually to love and sexual attraction for each other. An arranged marriage is based on this basic premise. This is what Hartfield and Rapson (1993) also argue in their Two-factor theory of love–the two requirements for falling in love are: socio-cultural background that paves the way for falling in love and an appropriate person in terms of appearance, personality, background, and values.

Although feelings might not be spontaneous and totally by free will, individuals condition themselves to fall in love and develop sexual interest in each other because of their dharma -- moral commitment to marriage. So great is the faith in the strength of the arranged marriage, it is believed emotional feelings for each other emerge out of this calculated social arrangement.

Love and sexual attraction are social constructions, managed by the parents and the extended family: they are not spontaneous, free-will acts as in the case of romantic marriages.

Arranged marriage challenges the notion that sexual attraction and love are prerequisites to sexual intimacy. In this study, some men and women believe that it is not necessary to have sexual attraction and love before the marriage as they are the latent functions of sexual relationship after the marriage.

"The experience of the first night sex brings couples closer and binds them together and then love develops... what holds two together is sex... love becomes stronger after the sexual union." One respondent, a professor commented, "prema (love) comes from kama (desire), kama comes from prema, if there is sexual satisfaction between the couple, it will generate love."

Perhaps considering sex as sacred, equal to the union of God and soul, binds the couples together. Instead of moving from sexual attraction and love to sexual intimacy, they move from sexual intimacy to love and sexual attraction. This again shows how the development of individuals' sexual behavior can be reversed by cultural script and social networks. Although sexual attraction and compatibility of prospective marital partners are not discussed openly, there is a quiet, deep understanding that sexual intimacy between newly married couples who may not be sexually attracted to each other before the wedding, creates immutable strong natural bonds. *"Sexual attraction somehow develops, because we know we have to be together till we die."*

Human beings' sexual arousal and sexual attraction to a particular person is determined by what John Money (1986), calls "love map"–a mental map that develops in childhood in response to interactions with family, friends and other experiences. He further argues as we grow up we develop a mental picture of an ideal lover with specific details of physiognomy, build, race and color including temperament and manners.

Indian parents quite often create this "love map" in their children and young people about the ideal marital partner they ought to marry by emphasizing the importance of similarities of caste and religion, physical attraction, color of the skin, temperament and manners. Prospective marriage partners may not spontaneously fall in love with someone of their choice, but because of the "love map" that is imprinted on their consciousness by their families, it is probable they will like and approve of the person they are marrying. Some men and women in this study commented, *"My husband {my wife} is very much like what my parents wanted me to marry."*

Parents and extended family plant the idea of a suitable mate into the minds of their marriageable age children by innuendos, bantering and direct suggestions. The idea of a "suitable boy" or "suitable girl" is cultivated, nurtured and reinforced and after some time the prospective mates begin, as W.I. Thomas states, to "define the situation as real, and it becomes real in consequences" (Thomas, 1966:301). This is how two men defined their situation:

"Ever since I was a young man, my mother kept on telling me that I should marry this girl... she kept telling me how beautiful she is, what a good girl she is ... and I ended up marrying her"; "no choice , but to fall in love... I had predetermined myself falling in love with her."

"In arranged marriage, parents and others will begin to talk and tease you about a girl you are going to marry quite constantly. Somehow they will make you get attached to the person... they implant the idea in the young

minds...it is for this reason I don't want anybody to tease my son, a dental surgeon, about a suitable girl."

There are some serious criticisms against the parents planting the idea in young people and managing the mate selection; one woman said,

"the elders brain wash you... they keep telling you this is the man you are going to marry... they frequently tease you about marrying him... they suppress your individuality... they impose their thinking on you and the `feeling' of sexual attraction is imposed on you."

In romantic love marriages, love is the reason for marriage, but in arranged marriages, marriage is the reason for love. Love is seen as a "silent partner" in arranged marriages, but economic reasons and parental authority are foregrounded in it, whereas, in Western type of marriage love is foregrounded and the economic aspects are silent partners (De Munck 1998:297). As one male economics professor put it aptly, *"Either you love and marry or marry and love, it is the same."*

3

WHAT REALLY HAPPENS ON THE "FIRST NIGHT"? OR DOES ANYTHING HAPPEN AT ALL?

"We consummated our marriage 20-25 days after the wedding day... there was no hurry... sex was not the foremost thing." (a female media official)

"It took 17 days after the wedding for us to have sexual intercourse because of lack of privacy." (a male engineer)

What might come as a surprise is that the majority of respondents of this study did **not** consummate their marriage on their "first night", but 7 days to two months after the wedding. Only 28% reported consummating their marriage on the first night. With the exception of a few, **all** consummated either at their parents' home or at their in-laws' homes. Going on a honeymoon is not the norm, but an exception, and even those who went on a honeymoon had already, or had tried to, consummate their relationship at home.

A brief note about the "first night" Hindu ritual. As mentioned earlier, the Hindu religion is a pro-sex religion that celebrates and considers sex as sacred and a sacrament and reminds people that it should not be trivialized. In addition, it shapes and regulates individuals' sexual life. A Hindu wedding is not complete without having a special sacred ritual to mark the consummation of the marriage. The ritual is scheduled at an auspicious time and day after the wedding, in consultation with the astrologers. The "first night," a highly ritualized event, might not be on the day of the wedding, but any day that the family considers astrologically befitting for the consummation. What needs to be stressed here is this–couples sexuality is controlled by socio-cultural molding. Further, the "first night" sets a defining moment in couples sex life– **now**, it is culturally appropriate to have sex. As Weeks discussing human sexuality says, society produces sexuality in complex ways through social practices and social definitions. "Sexuality only exists through its social forms and social organization." (2003:18)

Bride's and bridegroom's parents have different concerns about the "the first night." The former is concerned about the sexual potency of the bridegroom, his sexual satisfaction with their daughter and later on about her conception. Whereas, the groom's parents are concerned about the bride's virginity, their sexual compatibility and later on about her conception. The bride's and the groom's parents have keen interest in the success of the "first night"; the next day, parents and relatives greet the couple with the big question on their face- did it happen?, subtly observe the behavior of the newly married. *"Is there a glow on their faces?"* If they suspect that it was a successful consummation, both the parties are greatly relieved. In Indian families, any discussion on sex is a "no, no", but yet through bantering, innuendoes, teasing, clever and crafty digging of information from the young couple, the families try to find out about the success or failure of the "first night." If they suspect that there is a problem in the paradise, they hope eventually *"they will adjust to each other," "well, these things take time...you know."*

This chapter deals with the two groups, **The BEFORE-MARRIAGE GROUP AND THE AFTER-MARRIAGE GROUP'S** experience of consummation of the marriage. As it might be recalled, 49% of the total sample belong to the Before-Marriage Group. This group refers to the individuals who had sexual attraction, feelings of love, and some physical intimacy during the period of engagement or acquaintance before they got married, and the After-Marriage Group (46% of the total sample) refers to individuals who developed sexual attraction, interest, love and physical intimacy after they got married. The differences between the two groups in the experiences of "First Night" is striking. This striking difference seems to narrow in sexual satisfaction and compatibility, as the marital life progresses for both the groups.

THE BEFORE-MARRIAGE GROUP:

"We consummated on the wedding night. It was totally pleasant...both of us enjoyed and experienced orgasm the very first night... we thought orgasm is heaven."

(an experience of a couple who were both sexually attracted before the marriage)

As noted earlier, in spite of the fact arranged marriages are not based on romantic love and sexual attraction, 49% of the total sample reported having sexual attraction, feelings of love, and physical intimacy during the period of engagement or acquaintance before the marriage. There seems to be a high degree of correlation between the presence of sexual attraction and feelings of love, and a positive experience of the "first night". Approximately 58% of the male respondents and 47% of the female respondents who had experienced sexual attraction, physical intimacy, and feelings of love BEFORE the marriage also reported having a positive experience with their consummation. Positive experience refers to sexual enjoyment, satisfaction, compatibility, and orgasmic pleasure. Male and female's differential experience of orgasm will be discussed later on.

Most of the respondents of this group attribute the success of their consummation to the engagement period where they got emotionally, intellectually, and physically acquainted with each other. A man stressing the importance of acquaintance before the marriage, in agreement with many others, said:

"Our first night was a totally pleasant experience... six months of knowing each other helped us."

Respondents describe their positive experiences of the first night as: *"thrilling," "exciting," "totally positive," "unparalleled experience," "most blissful experience." Even after many years of marriage, a man still remembered his "first night" as a "memorable experience... both of us had orgasms many times that night... I made love to her six times that night."*

Socio-cultural similarities seem to lead to sexual attraction and enjoyment. As Michael et.al., the authors of *Sex in America* point out, even in a liberal society with individual freedom such as America, "We usually have sex with people who are remarkably like ourselves–in age, race, ethnicity, and education." (1994:44) This is nothing new to an ancient culture like India. A female professor who liked her husband, but was not very much sexually attracted to him before she got married to him, felt:

"My first night was a pleasant experience. I felt very familiar with him because of our similar backgrounds. Even though I didn't know him... I felt as though I have known him for several years. I was very comfortable with him the first night... never felt strange with him."

In spite of their mutual sexual attraction, most of the men and women of this group also did not consummate on the day of the wedding day because of lack of privacy or the family had not scheduled the ritual of "first night". Couples are separated and sequestered in their respective parents' home and not allowed to be intimate until the family schedules the ritual of the "first night."

Although female respondents of this group reported their consummation as a positive experience, even in this group only 29% of them experienced orgasm and sexual enjoyment when they consummated their relationship for the first time. The experience of these women in comparison with the majority of women who did not have sexual pleasure on the first night or even the first couple of months after marriage is striking. A professor of English literature, who was sexually attracted to her husband and had some physical intimacy with him before their marriage and also had sexual intercourse on the "first night" remembered,"*It was a very pleasurable experience. I experienced my first orgasm in life that day!"*

Another woman, a professor, in the same category describes her "first night" as, "I can't think of anything negative. *I looked forward to being with this man for a few months now... It was a memorable moment...I experienced my first orgasm... The next day I was very happy... I was satisfied... He was satisfied."*

This small percentage of the total female respondents, who reported experiencing orgasm the very first time they had sex with their husbands, had these special characteristics. They were strongly sexually attracted to their husbands, had fallen in love with their husbands, and they had a positive outlook on sex and were less inhibited. Privacy helped them to relax. Sex education from sex manuals, and the sexual knowledge they gained from their experienced friends and relatives facilitated their positive experience. Moreover, they were mentally prepared and were looking forward to their "first night". Comments such as these reveal the pleasurable experience of these women:

"I was mentally prepared for the first night, I didn't feel he was a total stranger... I experienced orgasm the first night... It was totally positive and enjoyable."

It may come as a big surprise that the majority in the **BEFORE-MARRIAGE GROUP** of females who reported sexual attraction and some intimacy before the marriage, 69% did not experience orgasm and other sexual enjoyments at the beginning. Although they felt sexual arousal towards their husbands, it was days or several weeks before they could experience it, for reasons such as lack of privacy, limited or no sexual knowledge, fears of sex, fear of pregnancy, sexual inhibition and embarrassment about sexual intimacy with their husbands at their parents' home. Women who had difficulty reaching orgasm while still staying at their parents' or in-laws home, were able to achieve it once they went on a honeymoon and moved into their own home. Women expressing their disappointment with their "first night" related:

"I didn't have much knowledge of sex, even though I was over 30... He didn't know about foreplay...or sex... I didn't get much satisfaction on the first night... I was uncomfortable looking at the nude male body... it bothered me."

Some women who were sexually attracted to their husbands as soon as they met and had some physical intimacy with him before marriage also had difficulty experiencing their orgasm. As one woman described,

"it took a month for me to have an orgasm... I had to educate my husband about arousing me."

Another professional woman seemed to have been disappointed with her experience of consummation; *"I was expecting an earth shattering event... It didn't happen. On the "first night," your senses are still not aroused, because you don't know much about sex."*

It is interesting to note that women who had an enjoyable "first night" felt that it was their husbands who were responsible for their positive first sexual experience, sexual awakening and enjoyment. They attributed their sexual satisfaction to their husbands' patience, affectionate behavior, and thoughtful and sensitive ways. In addition, they think their husbands' less sexually aggressive nature, their understanding qualities, their sexual arousal skills, and the sex education they provided, were all responsible for their sexual pleasure. While it may be true that the pleasing qualities of husbands play a decisive role in women's sexual enjoyment, it also suggests transferring sexual enjoyment responsibility to their husbands. To assume individual responsibility for sexual enjoyment may suggest sexual aggressiveness. A female businesswoman commenting on how her husband was responsible for her sexual awareness and enjoyment commented,

"He helped me to have a positive attitude... my orgasm was absolutely satisfying... it is feeling of oneness with God...the closest thing to experiencing paramathma (God)

Puri (1999:108), also noticed her female subjects attributed their sexual awakening and enjoyment to their husbands; "understanding husband" is the enabling factor in women's transition from sexual inhibition to enjoyment, she states.

Men, in return, also take pride in the fact that because of these above mentioned qualities, they were successful in bringing sexual pleasure to their wives and make them sexually compatible to them. **None** of the female respondents reported any case of "marital rape" on the first day of consummation, rather they refer to their husbands sexual approach to them as gentle, understanding, thoughtful, patient and inexperienced. Men substantiated women's report of their experience, by stating:

"I didn't force myself on her. I showed sexual interest but she was not ready, she was tired and puzzled... she had just then come to my home... it took 4-5 days after the wedding to consummate."

Women had developed positive attitudes towards sex with their husbands as a result of socialization and cultural conditioning. A female professor commented about the sociocultural construction of sexual attraction, desire and satisfaction: *"My first night was glorious! Indian girls are conditioned to think that they must have sex with their husbands, so they begin to think positively about their sexual experience with their husbands without having negative feeling about sex."* As Puri (1999) noted in her study, there is a belief among women she studied that sexual activity within a marriage is compulsory as it stabilizes the marriage and increases the emotional bond of love.

Many respondents who consummated their relationship at one of the parents' home, but went on a honeymoon after this, reported less satisfaction with their first night. A very small percentage of them, that is 11% of them, who consummated on their honeymoon reported a greater satisfaction than those who did it at home. Lack of privacy and embarrassment about marital intimacy in the presence of relatives are valid reasons for sexual restraint and strained sexual enjoyment. Respondents felt:

"Real enjoyment came later when we went on a honeymoon or when we moved in to our own home." (a female accountant)

"The honeymoon definitely helped us to enjoy sex, that is, four days after the wedding... there was no privacy at home... when we went on honeymoon, we became close to each other." (a male engineer)

"At home there was no privacy... after we went on a honeymoon, I started having sex... didn't have any problems then... " (a female teacher)

Those who had adequate privacy in their parents home had no complaints about their sexual enjoyment.

Anticipation is the spice of desire! Many men and women commented about the intensity of the pleasure they experienced on the "first night", as they had built this long anticipation towards it, deferring instant gratification of sex during their period of engagement. A man said:

"I liked the long anticipation of four months, I could have made love to my fiancée anytime, but wedding night is wedding night... it takes away the charm of the wedding night if you have sex before the wedding." "It was a glorious culmination of long expectation" said another man.

"We consider sex as sacred, waiting helped the mental preparation for sex," stated a woman.

Both the male and female respondents of this Before-Marriage Group also reveal a life-affirming, positive attitude towards sex, enjoyment of sexual pleasure, and enjoyment of the beauty of the male and female nude body. While it may be common for men to make complementary remarks about the female body, women also enjoyed looking at and admiring the nude male body. A female classical musician admiring her husband's nude body said,

"We often think a woman's body is beautiful...my husband's body is beautiful to look at."

A few women were uneasy or inhibited about looking at their husbands' nude body on the "first night," but most women were relaxed, and accepted the sexual act as part of life.

THE AFTER-MARRIAGE GROUP;

"Our first night was totally negative... long, tiring, ritual... It took eight months after marriage to get sexual pleasure." (a female bank official)

"My first night was not pleasurable. I am frigid, he is sexually potent.. our personalities didn't match." (a female professor)

"On the first night I was not successful.. it took a week.. she was too inhibited... afraid of the male body..." (a male physicist)

"The first night was not that good... I was too excited... she complained of pain... I couldn't enter... seven days after my first attempt, I was successful." (a male engineer)

Why is the experience of the **After-Marriage Group** of the first night negative? Simply put, they were not sexually attracted to their marital partners before marriage, did not have feelings of love, and did not have physical intimacy. In addition, they were not acquainted with each other before the "first night." Approximately 46% of the total respondents belong to this After-Marriage Group. They also report that their consummation experience was negative and even disastrous in some cases, thus suggesting a correlation between the absence of sexual attraction and a negative experience of the "first night."

A significant gender disparity is shown here– females formed 63% of the **After-Marriage Group,** whereas males formed 37% of the same group. The majority of The After-Marriage Group female respondents, that is 95% of them, but only 36% of the male respondents of the same group, reported dissatisfaction with their "first night." For men, a negative experience refers to unsuccessful consummation, delayed consummation, lack of sexual enjoyment; but for women, in addition to the aforementioned aspects they had fear, pain and inhibition about sex. A female physician noted, women complain of vaginal pain, *"because they are not physically sexually aroused... they are tense."*

But what is interesting is, although the majority of the **Before-Marriage Group** women experienced delayed sexual enjoyment of several days to weeks, it was sooner than the **After-Marriage Group** women. The latter group of women took even longer; that is, 2 to 6 months to experience orgasm. Many male respondents from both the groups, whose wives were not interviewed for this study, also reported that their wives experienced delayed sexual satisfaction that lasted from several weeks to several months.

The first time sexual experience of this group suggests, unlike the Before Group, the After Group members had to consummate their marriage even though there was a lack of sexual attraction and feelings of love between them. Sex was seen as fulfilling one's marital duty and expected behavior, rather than a spontaneous action based on sexual attraction. The wedding is over and the ritual of "first night" is completed, *"because we are married we must have sex, that was the idea in my head"* says a business woman who knew her husband only 17 days before the wedding. She was not sexually attracted to her husband before the wedding.

NONE of the respondents of this group consummated their marriage on the assigned day of the "first night', but took a longer time to consummate their marriage than the Before Group. It took anywhere from one week to six -eight weeks, depending on the comfort level of the partners. This group also took a longer time to experience the pleasures of sex than the Before Group, as indicated above. Many factors are associated with negative experiences of consummation of this group.

The delay in consummation and sexual satisfaction of this group could simply be attributed to their brevity of acquaintance, lack of sexual attraction, physical intimacy, and familiarity with each other before the wedding. These factors seem to determine sexual behavior. *"I met him 17 days before the wedding day... There was no time for me to think that I am sexually attracted to him...I liked him as a person but no sexual attraction... We consummated the marriage 15 days after the wedding. It was not much of an excitement because you really do not know what it is..."*

Absence of sexual attraction and inadequate sexual awareness made it difficult, especially for women to consummate their marriage, resulting in rejection of their husbands' sexual overtures. Having sex without sexual attraction or undeveloped sexual attraction, combined with inhibited sexual desire and absence of foreplay, results in inability for sexual arousal, results in pain, and a pleasureless sexual act. These women had not yet made an emotional connection with their husbands; an indispensable factor for women's sexual enjoyment. Such women remember their *"first night"* as *"horrible," "disastrous," "terrible," "shocking," "very painful."* One woman with a *"very successful marriage"* remembering her *"first night"* said, *"come to think of it, it (arranged marriage) is a brutal system."*

One woman describing her "disastrous" first night said:

"My husband asked me for a "sweet kiss" on the first night. I immediately got an aversion towards him... I drank milk and gave him milk and said I am tired, covered myself with a blanket and went to sleep." Another woman, who was not sexually attracted to her husband, but married him because she wanted to please her parents told him on the "first night," *"don't touch me, I am not sexually attracted to you."* Her new physician husband respected her wish and both of them slept in different beds on their honeymoon. A female engineer who was not sexually attracted to her husband who is a professor, remembers her "first night" experience as *"very painful and unenjoyable"* as her husband *"forced himself"* on her. It has to be noted here cases such as these are very few and not to be generalized as the experiences of a lot of people who have gone through an arranged marriage.

"If I would have known enough about sex, I would have been less apprehensive about sex," says a woman. In spite of the fact that the Hindu religion is a pro-sex religion, Indian society in general does not promote sex education or sexual awareness, leaving especially women in ignorance and fear of sex. The society is more concerned about religious wedding sexual rituals than sex education. A few liberal parents educate their children in sex education, but the vast majority of prospective marriage partners are not fully aware of sexuality and the sexual act. This inadequacy of sexual knowledge poses a problem for the newly married people, more so for the women.

In contradiction to the 29% of women of the Before-Marriage Group who had adequate knowledge of sex and sexual enjoyment on their "first night," women in this group reported having no or limited knowledge of sex. The sex awareness they had, came from censored western movies, friends, and novels and later from husbands. The majority of the women had not prepared themselves by reading sex manuals, but more men than women had read sex manuals, seen blue movies and learnt the techniques from their friends before the marriage. Only **six** people had read the *Kamasutra*.

A woman remembering about her absence of sexual attraction towards her husband and ignorance of sex said,

"The first night was a disaster... I did not know what to expect... I didn't know about the male anatomy... I was shocked... I was ignorant... I felt violated."

"I was afraid of sex because of the fear of pregnancy" says another woman.

"I had no idea about sex, that is why it was shocking to me... when my husband came on to me... I didn't know how to react."

The majority of men reported that their wives were ignorant about sexual matters and the burden fell on them to educate them, which they seemed to enjoy and take pride in. A man took pride in the fact that he was *"responsible for her (his wife's) sexual pleasure, aroused her, educated her... I had the pleasure of teaching sex to her..she was scared of sex, hesitant, shy." "I raised the sexual awareness in my wife... I enjoyed the whole process of initiating her and teaching her"* says a charted accountant. Women's coyness and sexual inexperience seem to turn on some men, giving them a special kind of sexual power over their wives.

Women felt that their ignorance of sex and mental unpreparedness resulted in shock and disgust on the first night. *"The First night was a shocking experience... I thought, he'll take some time before having sex... it happened so immediately, it was shocking... I was not mentally prepared."* Women did not know how to react, respond, and cooperate. Some women were quite shocked and bothered to see their husbands' aroused organ and felt a sense of disgust, and one even tried to 'calm' her husband by throwing cold water on his private part.

Although husbands had more sexual awareness than their wives, since both husbands and wives were virgins, with the exception of three, their sexual inexperience was a problem. Women felt that they suffered pain, discomfort and no sexual pleasure at the beginning because of their husbands' and their own inexperience. Husbands didn't know how to arouse their wives and also suffered from premature ejaculation.

"When he used to ejaculate quickly, there was no time to enjoy... because he was a virgin he did not know how to prolong...I wasn't satisfied," said a female T.V. program host.

A female teacher talking about the inexperience of her husband said:

"The first time it was quite awkward... there was a lot of fumbling... I didn't enjoy... had a splitting headache."

"He didn't know enough about sex... he didn't how to arouse me... took a long time, more than a year, to experience orgasm" reports another woman.

Premature ejaculation is considered as a sexual problem by Indian sex researchers and psychiatrists as indicated earlier. Although in this study, there is not adequate documentation of men suffering from premature ejaculation, it is considered a major problem with Indian males. R.H. Dastur, a Mumbai sexologist, the author of *Sex Power (1983)*, talks about premature ejaculation and impotence as the most common problems among married couples.

Some men also admitted their abysmal ignorance in sexual matters; they did not know how to arouse their wives or where to enter.

"I didn't know much about foreplay, I had not read sex manuals... I didn't know how to arouse her." (a media executive)

"We are not sexually educated... my friend couldn't enter into his wife... because his foreskin was not pulled back... he was not circumcised... he started

bleeding and had to see a doctor... this has happened to several of my friends." (a bank official)

A microbiologist also expressed how he lacked experience, skills and knowledge on how to sexually arouse his wife :

"I was too excited on my "first night"... It wasn't that good... It was too painful for her. I couldn't enter her... my mother, a physician asked me to use Vaseline (petroleum jelly). I tried to enter again... I couldn't... We just kissed and slept. I read sex manual again... I learnt how to arouse her. Seven days after the first attempt, we fully consummated."

Since preservation of virginity is highly acclaimed, women felt their sexual novice and low sexual awareness were important factors in their unpleasant experience of consummation. Furthermore the conflicting sexual scripts of society, created ambivalence and confusion among women regarding their sexual behavior.

"Sexual experience is highly discouraged before the wedding, but suddenly you are expected to give a great performance on the "first night"... women do not want to give the impression that they know about sex, lest husbands might think they are not virgins" said a woman.

Another woman felt if women are sexually uninhibited, *"it puts men off, especially in an arranged marriage... they think you are a fast woman."* Women are in limbo; they do not know whether they should enjoy the pleasures of sex or act "inhibited" and "ignorant", just to please and impress their husbands. There exists a dilemma between gaining personal pleasure and acting sexually appropriate that gives women social respectability. Furthermore, female virginity ensures not only trust in the marriage, but also for men it is a "feel good" matter for their ego; to feel *"she had kept 'it' for me"* helps in respecting their wives.

Many men in this study were pleased that they had married virgins, even though some of them felt the issue was unimportant, because they know that arranged marriage assures of virgin women. Men who considered virginity is a non issue felt," *it is not important at all after marriage... whether my wife was virgin or not didn't cross my mind. Why dig the past? What do you gain?"*

Those men who give importance to virginity before the marriage felt, *"I was happy she was a virgin... It gave me lot of satisfaction;" I was happy she was a virgin...it is very important she must only belong to me."*

Societal scripts about sexual behavior for girls stress the importance of "purity," just like Sita was pure in the classic Hindu epic *Ramayana*. When *Sita's* husband *Rama* blamed her for being polluted by his arch enemy *Ravana*, *Sita* vows her purity by jumping into the fire. But the gods rescue her and stamp divine proof of her innocence. Puri's (1999) analysis of narratives of middle and upper-class women also indicate premarital chastity as determined by normative prescriptions, is central to women's definition of sexual respectability.

Since the "First night" ritual was held at home, lack of privacy was seen as a recurring reason for difficulty in consummating the marriage and for impaired sexual enjoyment. Cramped homes, regular intervention of parents and relatives into young people's time and space, inaccessibility to an attached bathroom are barriers to the joy of sex. The issue of privacy bothered women more than men and was also connected with women's inability in achieving orgasm. Women began to enjoy orgasm when they left their parents or joint family home and started their own home.

> *"There was lack of privacy in my mother's place... cot was not comfortable... the bedroom was close to my brothers and sisters bedrooms... I didn't want to disturb them... I worried about my bangles and anklets making noise...what will they think?... I remember my first night as a negative experience."*
>
> *"I wanted to take the Pill before the consummation, but every time I tried to take... some relative was in my space, asking me "why are you taking an aspirin, aren't you well ?"...nine months later I had a baby!"*
>
> *"We had to spend a very hot night... the fan was not fixed... it was*

March and a lot of mosquitoes... after a long ritual we were very tired." (all female respondents)

"My parents house was a small one... we were afraid of others and our sounds... there was lack of privacy." (a male professor)

DO THE WEDDING AND "FIRST NIGHT" HINDU RITUALS HELP IN CULTIVATION OF SEXUAL ATTRACTION AND PRO-SEX ATTITUDE? OR DO THEY ACT AS BARRIERS TO SEXUAL ENJOYMENT?

As much as Indian society appears to be sexually inhibited, because people do not overtly display their sexual attitude or behavior, the Indian culture of sex creates an environment of sexuality that exerts influence on sexual behaviors. An ambience of physiological and psychological arousal is created on the First Night which is meant to create romantic attractions between marital partners who may or may not be sexually attracted to each other yet. As mentioned earlier, the family members schedule the "First Night" on an auspicious day and time after consulting the astrologers. The bride and the groom take a ritual bath, often helped by the older married female relatives before the sacred act of consummation. Couples offer *pooja* (prayer) for fertility and healthy and intelligent children.

The bridal chamber is filled with things that are believed to have aphrodisiac effect; a new bed is decorated with beautiful jasmines and other sweet smelling flowers. The intoxicating smell of incense, rose water and sandlewood and other perfumes permeate the room to entice and enhance sexual pleasure. Soothing little lamps light up the room. Almond milk with saffron or honey, delicious fruits, and protein-laden sweets prepared in pure ghee (clarified butter) are kept in the bedroom to increase the sexual appetite and potency of newly married couples. Classical music is played outside the bedroom to enhance the sexual enjoyment of the newly married couple. The "first night" doesn't give much privacy to the couples, rather it is an exuberant and joyful event with relatives and ubiquitous mosquitoes hovering over the couple. To add to this passion (if any) is the Indian heat!

Perhaps the explanation for how two strangers with some sexual attraction or no sexual attraction towards each other develop sexual attraction and feelings for each other may lie in the pro-sex attitude of Hindu religion. Similarities of marital partners along with the influence of Hinduism seem to generate sexual attraction. It is argued that sexuality is biological, but yet Hindu religion, cultural norms, sexual customs and families influence the sexual behavior of individuals. Sexuality in arranged marriages appears to be mainly a social construction. As Reiss (1986) and Kon (1987) argue, human sexual behavior is a social and cultural phenomena, and shared cultural scripts incite erotic arousal.

In this study, a majority of the respondents, that is, 68% of them, feel that the Hindu religion is a pro-sex religion and 52% of them feel that it has also created a positive attitude towards sex within the marriage. A male professor of Botany summed up:

> *"Hindu religion has a lot of sexual innuendoes... sexual symbols and sculptures and pictures of gods and goddesses in blissful sexual union, Shiva's linga (phallic symbol) inspire amorous feeling... they have an aphrodisiac effect... We don't find this in other religions."*

Although Indian parents do not generally discuss sex with their children, individuals are exposed to the great love stories of gods and their uninhibited enjoyable sex lives. Temples are laced with erotica in order to remind people sex is sacred and an integral part of one's life. What is interesting is, even the pendant in a chain that married women wear indicate the pro-sex attitude of Hinduism; in some castes women wear pendants that look like a pair of breasts and in another caste, the pendant looks like a vulva. Hinduism is filled with many sexual symbols.

Forty eight percentage of the respondents also feel that the Hindu wedding and the "first night" rituals created in them a romantic, sensuous feeling and stimulated mutual sexual interest and attraction.

As one male respondent put it;

"It (wedding rituals) was a kind of foreplay before foreplay."

The rituals acted as an ice breaker, lowering any sexual inhibition and mentally and physically prepared them for the first encounter of physical intimacy. It was especially beneficial to those who were unfamiliar with each other.

"Sexual feelings develop through wedding rituals... when you go through Sapthapadi (ritual of seven steps) and the ritual of pouring water over the coconut, the ritual of feeding sweets to each other... the pleasure and enjoyment you get from touching just the finger of your groom and holding hands for the first time is far superior to orgasm through sex" comments a female manager reflecting the opinions of others.

In another ritual game filled with symbols, a ring is dropped in the bowl of water, the bride and the groom are asked by the priest to retrieve it, whoever gets the ring first is considered as the domineering person in the marriage-- the point of this game, as others, is to slowly physically acquaint the couple with each other. Some respondents describe this particular "sex game" as *"sensuous," "thrilling," "like an electric current going thru' you"* as it was the very first time they touched each other.

As in all cultures, Indian culture too has its own set of objects, actions, erotic symbols and signals or "sexual codes," as Davenport (1977) calls them that are used to convey erotic or sexual meanings. These sexual codes influence sexual behavior and incite mutual sexual attraction.

An interesting "first night" ritual that is meant to shed the inhibition of a young couple, especially of the bride is the ritual of "changing sari in front of the groom"-- a bride is asked remove the sari (Indian women's garment) and wear another one in front of her groom. A male accountant talked about another fascinating sexual arousal ritual that is part of his family's customs:

"After our wedding we were made to stand outside the temple and made to bathe publicly in front of the relatives and guests. I was covered below the waist and my wife was fully draped in a sari. I poured the bath

water mixed with turmeric powder on my wife and she poured it on me... the wet sari clinging to my wife's body was sexy." The rain drenched sari clinging and defining the curvaceous beautiful and buxom body of the heroine is a recurring scene in many Bollywood movies!

Hindu wedding and "first night" rituals, as discussed earlier, is meant to act as external stimuli for the sexual arousal of the couples who are unfamiliar with each other sexually. From the time, the concept of marriage and the image of the persons whom they are going to marry enter their consciousness, couples begin to prepare themselves for the consummation. The sex on the "first night" is an anticipatory sex for the **Before-Marriage group;** it is a culmination of a long anticipation. As many respondents put it: *"I liked the long anticipation," "I didn't want to have premarital sex, because I wanted to build anticipation."* So with such anticipation, they enter the sexually enticing bridal chamber, and they respond to the sexual stimuli created by social customs. But, for the **After-Marriage Group,** this external stimuli does not seem to have much effect, as they were not sexually attracted to each other before the wedding. For this group, the "first night" ritual is just a ritual.

Delamater (1991:50) argues that emotional experience involves arousal and cognition--the *Two-factor theory.* It is argued sexual arousal is a reaction to external stimuli and when the individuals experience arousal, they cognitively process the information and attribute the arousal to stimuli. "It is the attribution that defines their emotions." We do not know whether arranged marriage couples are reacting to the sexual stimuli in the bridal chamber or the couples themselves act as sexual stimuli to each other or a combination of both. But the couples interpretation or attribution of these social customs that act as sexual stimuli defines their emotions.

Simply put, the couples who are sexually unattracted and unfamiliar with each other, now, with the help of social customs that act as sexual stimuli, are able to interpret that they are sexually attracted to each other. "I marry, therefore I am sexually attracted" or as a female respondent put it, *"because we are married, we must have sex, that was the idea in my head",* seem to be the self-conditioning the couples go through. Once the couples come to realize that they are marrying each other, the haunting sex thoughts and sexual fantasy enter into their consciousness. These sex thoughts in the form of innuendoes and bantering are planted into their minds by relatives, friends, and customs of the society. Sexual attraction is cultivated and conditioned.

"Hindu rituals are like fossils" (a male scientist).

About 25% of the sample felt that the rituals were a nuisance and an obstruction to a successful "first night" and 27% had no opinion on the subject. One dysfunction of Hindu wedding and first night rituals is that they are exhausting, demanding and time-consuming. The bride and the groom are given a ritual bath, then they have to endure a series of wedding rituals as mentioned earlier sitting in front of the holy fire, then they have to greet hundreds of guests while standing and when this is all over, they have to go through the "first night" ritual.

"On the wedding day you have to get up early... 3:30 a.m. for the long ritual bath and poojas (prayers), the previous night you are kept awake because of poojas... we are also asked to fast... (believed to be good for sexual activities) again you have to go through "first night" rituals... by the time you go to the bedroom... it is not possible to have sexual appetite... your legs feel weak... you are exhausted."

By this time the young couples are so exhausted and irritated that as some men and women mentioned, *"they preferred to sleep rather than making love"*.

Individuals critical of the Hindu rituals feel that the consummation of marriage is heavily scripted and controlled by the elders. A medical representative criticizing the excessive ritual said, *"The elders are not interested in our sex life."*

"On the nuptial day, my father-in-law gave me sex education. He asked me to have intercourse at 3.a.m... he told me to have sex only during this time, as it is an auspicious time, and not to do it any other time." (a male professor

of religion)

"Long, tedious, hot, and tiring rituals" are impediments to a successful "first night" and sexually enjoyment, say the critics of the rituals.

"Too many rituals... they didn't incite sexual interest in or attraction towards my husband... the whole thing was irritating to me... there was no privacy... the elders had arranged the "first night" ritual eight days after the wedding !" (a female professor).

"I didn't like the "first night" ritual.. it was very embarrassing with elders outside your bedroom... It took 4 days to consummate the marriage... even then I couldn't succeed with my wife." (a male microbiologist).

There are some cases in this study where the parents and other older relatives scheduled the "first night," several months or even one year after the wedding day. Concerns about inauspicious time and unwanted pregnancy that may derail the studies or professional advancement of the young couple are given as the reasons.

A male professor of economics in this study, who was sexually attracted to his wife before the marriage and also had fallen in love with her, talking about this problem stated:

"There was a one-year gap between the wedding day and the "first night"... because I was a student, the elders postponed it for fear of pregnancy... I didn't question... It (sex) would have distracted my attention from my studies. Sex is distractive."

"During this period of one year of waiting for the "first night" ritual, we developed deep intimacy... we slept together... fondled, caressed, but no sexual intercourse... my wife didn't want to consummate without the first night ritual... she felt it was not proper... I never forced her... I was very frustrated."

Superstitious fears about myths surrounding sexual intercourse and conception during evil constellation of stars, moonless nights and the full moon, and festival of gods and goddesses prevent young couples from consummating and enjoying their sexual pleasure. Older female relatives use this cultural injunctions to monitor the sex lives of the newly married. A male medical representative in this study reported:

"They didn't allow us to go out of house for 3-4 days after the wedding because of the fear that evil spirits may strike us. They did some "shastra" (religious ritual) to protect us. During "ashada," (inauspicious season) she was sent to her mother's home. After she came back, we consummated our marriage...I had sex with my wife four to six weeks after the wedding."

Such is the invasive power of the culture and interference of the family elders that young passionate couples have to discipline their sexual urges for a long time. Some may even have consummated their marriage not because they had a great urge or passion, but because an auspicious day was set up for the big event. Consummation can take place only on the "first night" legitimized by the Hindu ritual and approved by the astrologers and the female elders of the family. So strong is the social and cultural control of sexuality that biological impulses become subservient to the influence of social norms.

What happens if the elders do not make arrangements for the "first night"? In one case, a timid couple with sexual inhibitions had not made any honeymoon arrangements on their own, assuming the elders would make the "first night" plans and the elders assumed the young couple had made their own plans. After the wedding, they looked sadly into each others' eyes without having the courage to say, "let us spend the night together." So they ended up sleeping with their respective families in separate locations far from each other! The family and couples were too focused on the wedding arrangements and gifts and nobody paid attention to the most significant night in a couple's married life.

It is worth mentioning here, in addition to the two mentioned groups--Before-Marriage Group and After-Marriage Group, there is a negligible number of men and women who had no sexual attraction and familiarity with their new marital partners, had met just once before the wedding, but their consummation was "fantastic" by their own account, that included orgasmic pleasure and enjoyment of each other without much inhibition. They said their behavior was driven by natural instincts and it was culturally expected behavior to consummate the marriage. A woman explained this behavior by attributing it to *"mind conditioning of girls that they should have sex with their husbands on their "first night", so she thinks positively about sex..."*

In conclusion, a few major points, differences and similarities between the **THE BEFORE-MARRIAGE GROUP** and **THE AFTER-MARRIAGE GROUP** may be noted here:

To stress again, there is a significant difference in male and female experience of sexual enjoyment. A higher percentage, (63%) of male respondents of both the groups-- the **Before** and the **After Group** had a positive experience when they consummated their marriage and reported no delay in sexual satisfaction and enjoyment; whereas, 71% of the total female respondents including both the groups experienced delayed sexual satisfaction and enjoyment. Men's sexual satisfaction appears to be related to their own sexual urges and sexual arousal to the visual experience of female body, whereas women's delay in sexual satisfaction is related to the limited or absence of emotional connection to their husbands. Only 29% of the total female respondents (including both the groups) reported excellent sexual enjoyment and experienced orgasm the very first time they consummated their marriage.

In both the groups, as indicated earlier, women experienced delayed orgasm by several weeks to months, but many **Before-Marriage Group** female respondents seem to have experienced their orgasm sooner than **After-Marriage Group** female respondents. Perhaps, presence of sexual attraction, period of acquaintance, knowledge of sex, and less inhibition facilitated the early orgasm of the Before-Group women.

Based on the responses of the **Before-Marriage Group** and the **After-Marriage Group,** it may be possible to conclude that the former had higher levels of satisfaction and sexual pleasure on the "first night" than the latter, because of their sexual attraction and feelings of love towards their partners.

The intimacy and romantic feelings they developed during the engagement certainly helped the Before-Group to have sexual enjoyment.

Although, both the group members have married individuals like themselves, similarities of marital partners in the Before-Marriage Group appears to have played a crucial role in mutual sexual attraction and satisfaction on the "first night." Perhaps, the shared similarities of the After-Marriage Group members also help them in having sexual attraction and enjoyment, as the couples start their married life. Pines (1999) after analyzing findings from many studies on romantic attraction, concludes that similarities such as, religion, education, economic, social and physical, play a key role in sexual attraction and marital satisfaction.

The absence of privacy or inadequate privacy is a dominant issue with both the groups; 68% of the total sample felt, in general, it is an impediment to the successful consummation of marriage and sexual enjoyment. Privacy refers not only to the inconvenient position of the couples' bedroom and lack of space, but also to the intervention by the well-intentioned parents and extended family into couples' sex life and freedom. This may be an isolated case, nevertheless a female physician reported how her over possessive in-laws joined her and her husband (their only son) on their honeymoon trip!

The **Before-Marriage Group,** who were sexually attracted to each other, had feelings of love for each other, and had some physical intimacy with each other, had **less** complaints about these problems. Although the same problems were there, including relatively less privacy, but unlike the **After-Marriage Group,** they did not perceive them as serious enough to be detrimental to their sexual enjoyment. Perhaps because of their mutual sexual attraction, they were oblivious to these issues. As an adage goes, "When two people are in love, they can sleep on a razor edge"

Only **11%** of the **total** sample consummated their marriage on a honeymoon, but an overwhelming majority had to do the same at home after the "first night" ritual. Herein lies the major reason for delayed consummation and sexual enjoyment.

Eighty-nine percent of the total sample of males were informed about sex through sex manuals, novels, pornographic movies, and friends. Whereas, 59% of the total sample of women were informed about sex mainly through friends and older female siblings and cousins.

Women in both the groups had a higher level of ignorance about sex than males, but women in the **Before-Marriage Group** seemed to be better educated about sex than the **After-Marriage Group** women. The former had a positive attitude towards sex and were less inhibited than the After-Marriage Group.

Men and Women in the Before-Marriage Group had more sexual enjoyment than After-Marriage Group, simply because they were sexually attracted to each other and seem to have had more privacy than the After-Marriage Group or their sexual desire for each other surpassed the issue of privacy. This difference in sexual enjoyment between the groups stands out!

Men and women in both the groups were virgins with the exception of a few.

Women in the Before-Marriage Group attribute their sexual enjoyment to their husbands' consideration, sensitivity and sexual arousal skills. Whereas husbands of the women in the After-Group seem to be missing these qualities. Perhaps the difference was also because they were not sexually attracted to their husbands at the beginning.

In conclusion, one can argue sexual attraction, feelings of love, a romantic period of engagement, and mutual familiarity may facilitate an enjoyable "first night" and avoidance of months of delayed sexual satisfaction.

In the next chapter, an assessment of the marital life of BOTH the groups is attempted with the main focus on the sex lives of individuals after many or several years of marriage. A comparison of the **Before-Marriage Group** and **After-Marriage Group** may reveal whether sexual attraction is a pre-requisite for a good marriage. Is there a significant disparity in the quality of marital life between After-Marriage and Before-Marriage groups ? Does the Before-Marriage Group have a better marriage and a better sex life than the After-Marriage Group, who did not have sexual attraction before they got married ?

4

IS THERE SEXUAL SATISFACTION AND COMPATIBILITY IN ARRANGED MARRIAGES?

The data of this study on sexual satisfaction and compatibility show that:

88% of the total sample (including **both** the groups) who had arranged marriage report moderate to high satisfaction with their sex lives. To be specific, 63% reported that they are very satisfied with their sex lives and 25% reported moderate satisfaction. On a scale of 1-10, individuals who are very satisfied with their sex life graded themselves with a score ranging from 7-10; moderately satisfied people graded themselves with a score ranging from 4-6; and the unsatisfied graded themselves with a score ranging from 0-3.

80% of the total sample think that they are physically and emotionally involved in their sexual acts with their spouses.

The majority of female respondents reported delayed sexual satisfaction and pleasure. That is, 71% of the female respondents experienced their first orgasm 1-3 months after their first night; a few women took nearly 8 months to experience their first orgasm and only 29% women have experienced orgasm from their first night.

The majority of male respondents reported that they began to experience orgasm from the beginning of their married sex life. Even the small number of males who experienced delayed orgasm, experienced it earlier than their wives and other female respondents of this study.

"I have never experienced orgasm." Two women reported that they are frigid and only one woman reported her husband is impotent. Lack of sexual attraction and low sex drive are the given reasons.

Diversity in sexual practices, that is varied sexual positions, are reported by 52% of the total sample and 37% of the total sample report practicing oral sex. Higher number of males prefer oral sex than females.

Only 12% of the total sample report no satisfaction with their sex life.

WHY IS THERE SUCH A HIGH RATE OF SEXUAL SATISFACTION DESPITE AN ARRANGED MARRIAGE?

Marriage is anterior to love and sex in arranged marriages, unlike romantic marriages. There is an overwhelming feeling among the respondents that socio-economic similarities between two marriage partners leads to sexual attraction and love, and then on gradually to sexual satisfaction and compatibility. Similarities between marital partners are mutually rewarding. The greater the socio-economic similarities between marital partners, the greater their marital satisfaction, because of their similar attitudes, beliefs and expectations.

"We felt comfortable with each other," "I felt as though I have known him/her for a long time," "similarities and personality compatibilities lead to sexual compatibilities and satisfaction" are recurring comments.

Sexual behavior becomes a reciprocity behavior: *"He/she gives me a lot of sexual pleasure: I must give him/her the same pleasure." "Sex binds couples together... it holds them together,"* says a male professor of economics. Once couples are married, they have to "work" on finding each other sexually attractive; their mutual sexual attraction is a product of social construction. Husbands begin to see their wives as sexually attractive and their wives begin to respond to their husbands in the same manner, then husbands give them sexual satisfaction and wives reciprocate it (vice versa). These variables;

reciprocity of love and need satisfaction terms identified by Pines (1999) may influence sexual satisfaction in arranged marriages.

Sexual pleasure perpetuates sexual pleasure; it is cumulative. Once couples start experiencing sexual pleasures, it brings them closer and it also becomes addictive. *"Once we began to have sex, we began to enjoy it, sex brought us together... we became compatible sexually."* It is the sexual pleasure that is experienced that triggers mutual sexual attraction and satisfaction.

What is revealed is that sexual satisfaction, like sexual attraction, is a social construction; couples create it, cultivate it, condition it. Couples define their interaction should be sexual, which in turn influences their emotions and behavior, thus responding to each other's sexual cues resulting in sexual arousal.

"Before I didn't like sex, I was not experiencing orgasm. NOW I have real sexual urges for him. Before I used to think "what is this (sex) nonsense? I used to think I have to go to sleep next to him, now the punishment will start... then he made me feel comfortable. I have improved tremendously... I have experienced the ultimate joy of sex with my husband."

Sexual practices and enjoyment are not only directed by their biological impulses, but also by societal scripts. Schwartz and Rutter (1998:25,26) after analyzing many research studies on sexual behavior take the Integrative approach in explaining it. They suggest both biological and social context are central in understanding human sexuality. "Hormones are the cart, not the horse"; sexuality is influenced by cultural, personal and situational factors. Married couples in an arranged marriage are driven by the horse–the invasive culture. Couples are expected to work on their sexual satisfaction and sexual compatibility; marriage dissolution based on low sexual satisfaction is not socially acceptable.

The majority of the respondents report moderate to high satisfaction with their sex lives. How is it possible in an arranged marriage, where the marriage decision is not heavily influenced by sexual attraction ?

Although sexual desire may be primarily biologically determined with physiological and neurological factors playing a key role, cultivation of sexual attraction and desire may be influenced by socialization. In the Indian cultural scenario, children grow up with the notion that they should marry within their caste and have sex with members of the same or similar caste. Hence, as Delamater (1987, 249) argues, individuals are likely to develop sexual preference and sexual desire to "certain persons and behaviors." As a result of socialization, not only are couples likely to develop sexual desire to certain persons, but also find sexual satisfaction with that certain person. Sexual satisfaction then, one may argue, is acquired and cultivated or as Gagnon and Simon (1973) argue, sexuality is a sociocultural construction.

It is noticed in this study that expectations of the sexual aspect of marital life are realistic, pragmatic and balanced. The majority of the respondents also revealed that they would stay in their marriage, even if their sex life is not satisfying. *"Sex helps in enjoying life... it is part of life, but not the only thing in life... it helps in releasing my tension"* says a professional female. Sex as a minor component of marriage acts as a glue for the mutual attachment of couples. A female respondent put it succinctly about the importance of sex, *"sex is secondary in an arranged marriage."*

A male professor in agreement with many others think, *"Sex or sexual attraction is not the main criterion... we stay in the marriage because your wife is a ardhangi (the other half)."* Sexual attraction and joy of sex are not considered as the main purpose of marriage by most respondents, rather it is considered as only one of the important components of marriage. This is consistent with the Hinduism's views on marriage; *kama*, the sexual pleasure is only one of the aims of Hindu marriage. *Dharma* (fulfillment of religious obligations or moral duty) and *praja* (progeny) are more important than *kama*. But some Hindu scholars interpret that all three aims should be in balance.

Although many respondents report a satisfying sex life in arranged marriages, yet it appears, the attitude towards marital sex is pragmatic which Lee (1977) considers as "pragma love." Pragma lovers are practical about sexuality. Hence, this complaisance and lower expectations of one's sexual pleasure and compatibility may result in feeling satisfied with their sex lives.

The pro-sex attitude of Hinduism, that affirms the celebration of sex and the wedding promise of giving *kamache* (sexual pleasure) to each other are important factors in sexual satisfaction. The idea that *"sex is sacred"* is ingrained in Hindu consciousness. It is *dharma*, a marital duty, to perform sexual acts and to give sexual pleasure to each other; to be married is to have sex. A male bank officer, commenting on how Hindu religion creates romantic sensuous atmosphere for sex, commented:

"I think sex in the night begins in the morning... when we do pooja (prayers) in the morning, men are bare-chested... it is a turn on for wives.... When I see my wife dressed in a silk sari, jewelry and flowers... the sound of her dangling bangles and ankles while doing pooja... that is sexually enticing."

A male professor of physics said, *"Hindu religion has influenced us to have a positive attitude towards sex... an enjoyable sex life... sex is the purpose of marriage I have had a great contented sex life." " The lives and loves of the great lovers Shiva and Parvathi create positive healthy attitude towards sex... we have to enjoy everything,"* comments a female lecturer. A woman was reminded by her mother to *"remember God when you have sex."* An officer is an insurance company felt *"sex is beautiful... you feel refreshed and ready to take on the things the next day... mentally ready to solve the problems."*

General patterns of sexual behavior and sexual satisfaction:

There are some similarities and general patterns noted in the sexual behaviors of both After-Marriage and Before-Marriage group members of this study.

Happy marriages seem to have a happy sex life; individuals who are generally happy with their marriages also reported they have enjoyable and satisfying sex lives. In fact, in their responses, they use *"good marriage"* and *"good sex life"* synonymously. In Chand's (1989) inquiry into the factors responsible for a successful marriage in India, men and women in her study with high marital success also indicated high sexual satisfaction, and vice versa.

Most couples transform their sex lives dramatically after marriage; from lack of or some sexual attraction to mutual sexual attraction, from a less satisfying sex life to a very satisfying sex life, from being a sexual novice to sexually experienced, from total sexual inhibitions to complete liberation, from having no love making skills to a sophisticated lover. What is especially striking is the metamorphosis of females.

A female bank employee, who was *"never"* sexually attracted to her husband before marriage talked about the transformation in her sexual behavior:

"I found sex disgusting and dirty, but my husband was patient and considerate... he is very nice to me... I like him very much... he sexually awakened me and aroused me. My attitude towards him helped me sexually... I am very satisfied with my sex life."

A female media official's transformation is impressive too. She was not sexually attracted to her husband when she married, never had physical contact with her husband before the marriage. She recalled her first night was a *"horrible night." "I didn't cooperate with him sexually, I didn't allow him to touch me...but he was very gentle and very understanding... kind... these qualities made me feel sexually attracted to him. Now after more than 20 years of marriage... we both enjoy oral sex and I give myself 8 or 9* (on sexual satisfaction scale of 1-10).

"I like various sexual positions... I like to ride my husband 1-2 times a week... I am happy with my sex life," says another woman.

"I enjoy sex more ... as time went on I have begun to enjoy sex more... my inhibition is gone now" states a female teacher.

A male executive talked about his wife's sexual transformation in their 8 years of marriage. *"My wife used to reject me sexually often...she found ejaculation dirty... she was very inhibited... but now she enjoys different positions, oral sex and she wants sex in the afternoon! You have to be patient and cooperative... I have solved our sex problem."*

Another man talked about how sexually aggressive his wife has become, *"Quite often she wants to come on my top.... She enjoys this, but gets on my nerves." "Earlier her sexual response was not good... now she gives me suggestions for improvement of our sex lives... sometimes I am surprised by her requests.... She wants to give oral sex and receive it... she wants to come on my top... she wants to have it for a longer time"* says a bank official.

"I enjoy sex more now. I give credit to my husband." Many women attributed their sexual awakening and enjoyment to their husbands' patience, consideration, understanding, sensitivity and their sexual skills. In some cases, their husbands encouraged them to watch pornographic videos with them, which especially improved the sexual relations and enhanced their enjoyment. This is in agreement with Puri's (1999) study, who reports most of her female subjects like watching pornographic videos with their husbands as they act as stimulus to sexual activity and improve their sexual techniques and enjoyment.

"My husband always waits for me to climax first... then he climaxes... it has been like this for the last 20 years." Husbands' sensitivity is a big turn on for women; it is sexually enticing to them. "During *the first year it took a long time for me to come to orgasm. But my husband was patient, tender, tried to see I got satisfied... He waited patiently for 2 years for my chemistry to click towards him... He is very sensitive"* reports a school teacher.

What the above narratives suggest **again** is the role of an *"understanding," "gentle," "caring," "patient"* husband in women's sexual enjoyment. It may be recalled the same attributes of a husband are also responsible for women reporting sexually satisfying consummation of their marriage. Puri (1999:120) argues that "... understanding husband is vital to accounts of sexual pleasure" and women are less likely to report sexual dissatisfaction, because "to do so would be a reflection on the quality of their husbands, their marriage, and their lack of pleasure."

Women in **Before-Marriage Group** may have experienced their sexual pleasures earlier than **After-Marriage Group,** nevertheless, delayed sexual satisfaction and pleasure are quite common among women of both the groups. Whereas, men in both the groups reported no serious delays or problems with their experiencing orgasm. This finding is no different from Laumann et.al (1994); women are less likely to have orgasm than men in their American sample.

Why do women have delayed pleasures of orgasm? They take a considerable amount of time to shed their sexual inhibitions taught during their socialization. Girls are expected to remain virgins, control their sexual urges, dress modestly and not to display their sexuality or show they are interested in sex. *"If I show more sexual response, I was afraid he'll think that I had past sexual experience"*, says a lecturer in Botany.

Lack of sex education and experience of premarital sex, and fear of pregnancy act as hindrances too. More women than men are bothered about lack of privacy; a woman who had difficulty experiencing orgasm felt, *"I was too conscious of my surrounding parents.... In-laws... what will they say"?*

"I feel I must give him pleasure whether I like or not".

Women are expected to give pleasure rather than receive pleasure. Their subservient role in sexual acts may lead to fear of complaining about their not receiving pleasures. Even an expression of sexual dissatisfaction and requesting their husbands to stimulate them may be seen as unfeminine and sexually aggressive behavior. As women say, *"we are brought up like that... to control ourselves sexually, suddenly we can't change... it takes a long time to get adjusted sexually and experience the pleasures."* To liberate oneself from the premarital socio-sexual restriction imposed upon them takes considerable time.

The social constraints women are subjected to have an influence on their orgasm, overriding their biological capacity (Schwartz and Rutter 1998). But the good news is, with the exception of a few women, all the women of this study, **learned** how to have orgasm not only by experiencing the pleasures of sex, but also with the help of their sexually skillful and cooperative husbands.

Women report that their husbands also learned how to arouse them in due course of time; *"my husband didn't know how to arouse me... now he has improved a lot."* As Fisher (1992) and medical science have revealed, women tend to experience orgasm when they are physically and emotionally relaxed and with men who are sexually attentive and in a committed relationship.

Women may experience delayed orgasm after they get married, but their description of this awesome experience (when they begin to experience) is no different from men's. Contrary to the impressions that in an arranged marriage, women may not be experiencing the joy of sex and may not be enthusiastically sexually active with their husbands, the narratives suggest, the joyful sex life, pro-sex attitude and the sexually assertive behavior of women. Puri's (1999) findings reinforce this study's views that women are not exactly passive agents in marital sex life, rather they enjoy the emotional intimacy and sexual pleasure with their husbands.

Here is how women describe their experience of orgasm:

"It is absolutely satisfying it is like feeling of oneness or union with God... since we don't know what that experience with God is... this is the closest thing to it."

"I can't explain in words... you feel that this is what you are born for... total satisfaction... feel fulfillment in life."

"I felt I gained everything."

"It is an inner happiness."

"It is like getting lost somewhere and forgetting one's surrounding."

"It is an extraordinary feeling that cannot be compared to anything else."

"It is out of this world experience."

"I don't hear a thing."

These accounts of sexual enjoyment of women challenge Kakar's (1989) depressing portrayal of middle class women as sexually joyless, unsatisfied and inhibited people with limited zest for enjoying sexual pleasures.

Men report;

"it is Brahhmananda" (divine ecstasy)

"it's the peak of enjoyment... total contentment"

"it's fantastic.. the expressions on our faces

"an indescribable pleasure"

"orgasm is heaven"

"it is like electric current"

"it is an out of this world experience"

"it is blissful"

Although most women stated that they do not provide sex for their husbands as a marital duty, but yet 30% of the women admitted that they do so. *"I feel it is my duty to satisfy him... he is very nice to me;" "I used to feel I couldn't say no to him because I am the only one he could have it with."* Indian cultural expectations that women should be self-sacrificing and subordinate their wishes and interests to their husbands may shape their attitude in bed. Not a **single** male stated that his sexual behavior with his wife is based on marital duty.

Men and women had different interpretations of their sex lives; less frequent sex, lack of sexual interest and sexual inhibitions of wives are some of the common criticisms. Although couples have reciprocal oral sex, higher number of men than women enjoy oral sex. Higher number of women than men are inhibited about making love with the lights on and clothes off, and practicing diversity in sexual positions. A few women reported that they have never performed sex in total nudity or seen their husbands in total nudity, expressing fear of the intimidating male nude body. All these factors may be related to lack of privacy and sexual inhibitions.

Some women felt that their husbands get more pleasure out of sex than them: *"I don't experience sexual pleasure... my husband is selfish... he gets his pleasure;" "My husband enjoys sex more than me... he is in heaven."* There is also the issue that some husbands are indifferent after the sexual act and not appreciative: *"he enjoys it... I just please him... he is selfish... he never says pleasant things to me after sex, he rolls over to the other side and sleeps... I feel used and humiliated."* Women who are displeased with their husbands sexually are also the ones, who do not have sexual attraction towards their husbands or their sexual urges or interest are limited.

But all in all, most respondents think that their sex life is satisfying and compatible: *"all the factors are compatible including sex even though I didn't know her sexually before the marriage... I have no regrets about arranged marriage,"* says a bank official reflecting the opinions of most subjects of this study.

What turns men and women on sexually ? Most males are sexually aroused by, according to their order of priority; by breasts, curvaceous *deriere*, well-defined lips, waist, *"the sensuous rustle of silk sarees"*, *"long, braided, black hair dancing on the hips"*. Whereas females are turned on by the *"hairy chest"* and the *"total man."*

Only three women are alleged to be frigid by their own admission and one woman reported that she discovered that her husband was impotent on the wedding night. These individuals' sexual experience from the "first night" is fraught with problems and the problems persisted through their marital life, mainly because of their absence of sexual attraction towards their spouses and sexual incompatibility. But, since they do not see sexual satisfaction as the main aspect of their married life, lack of sexual enjoyment is not considered as a reason for divorce.

These women had never experienced orgasm with their husbands, and concealed this personal pain from their husbands without any discussion about it. Above all they protected the ego of their husbands and the marital harmony and stability, by mechanical motion of sex and faking orgasm. These women reported that they perform sex with their husbands as a wifely duty.

One of these women, a business woman who had premarital sex with a man with whom she was deeply in love but could not marry him because of her parents opposition to the inter caste marriage commented,

"I just go through it mechanically... I have never had orgasmic pleasure with my husband... he is a very good man... I consider sex as a duty... one has to love a person in order to experience sexual pleasure."

Another woman who had a traumatic experience with her impotent husband has this to say,

"it was a nightmare... he would excite me, but couldn't penetrate... he would go to the bathroom and come back and try again... for two years it went on like this, everyday after 9 p.m., I used to get fever, dreading that night."

She divorced her husband and remarried. Since premarital sex is highly disapproved of, until after the consummation, one is not sure about sexual compatibility and sexual problems individuals might have.

DOES THE BEFORE-MARRIAGE GROUP HAVE HIGHER SEXUAL SATISFACTION AND COMPATIBILITY THAN THE AFTER-MARRIAGE GROUP?

(Note: the Before-Marriage Group refers to the respondents who had sexual attraction, feelings of love and intimacy before the marriage and the After-Marriage Group did not have the same experience.)

There is a marked difference between the above groups in sexual satisfaction and compatibility:

82% of the **Before-Marriage Group** reported that they are **very** satisfied with their sex lives, but only 13% reported moderate satisfaction.

40% of the **After-Marriage Group** reported that they are **very** satisfied with their sex lives and 40% reported moderate satisfaction.

20% of the **After-Marriage Group** reported **no** satisfaction with their sex lives, whereas, a negligible number of the **Before-Marriage Group** reported the same.

A comparison of males in **both** the groups suggests there is not a significant difference between them in sexual satisfaction, whereas, higher percentage of women in After-Marriage Group, that is 24%, reported no satisfaction, whereas negligible percentage of women in Before-Marriage Group reported the same.

Not a single male reported dissatisfaction in his sex life in the Before-Marriage Group and only **one** male reported the same in the After-Marriage Group.

A positive correlation is found in the **Before-Marriage Group:** higher number of the respondents who had developed sexual attraction before their marriage, also reported diversity in sexual practices, both in sexual positions and oral sex. Whereas, low or absence of sexual attraction before the wedding seems to be correlated with a lack of diversity in sexual practices in the **After-Marriage Group.**

A few factors emerge as the reasons for low sexual satisfaction and low sexual compatibility in the After-Marriage group.

An outstanding reason is that the After-Marriage Group was not sexually attracted to their future marital partners before their wedding. In comparison to the Before-Marriage Group, they also reported that they give less importance to sex in marital life. Men think frigidity and sexual inhibition of wives contribute to their low satisfaction. Lack of privacy, differences between spouses in sex drive, lower expectations of sexual pleasure, and fear of pregnancy are also some of the explanations for their low satisfaction.

A striking difference is the After-Marriage Group took a longer time than the Before-Marriage Group, to develop sexual attraction to their marital partners and to experience sexual enjoyment and compatibility. Nevertheless, even for the After-Marriage Group, sexual satisfaction and compatibility improved with time. Although they report lower sexual satisfaction than the

Before- Marriage Group, most of them still consider their marriage successful. After a lengthy period of marital life, they seem to catch up with the Before-Marriage Group who were sexually attracted to each other before their wedding. The difference between the groups appears to taper off.

Presence of sexual attraction and feelings of love before the marriage are the stated reasons for higher sexual satisfaction and sexual compatibility in the **Before-Marriage Group.** This group seems to give more importance to sexual enjoyment and also have a more positive attitude towards sex than the **After-Marriage Group.** Compatibility of personalities, considerate, caring and loving nature of spouses, and sensitivity of husbands are other reasons given for high sexual satisfaction in the Before-Marriage Group. Lack of privacy is a not a great issue with this group. Most of the men didn't complain about their wives being sexually inhibited. It seems in general this groups think they have a good marriage; and a good marriage leads to good sex.

BARRIERS TO SEXUAL ENJOYMENT AND SATISFACTION IN ARRANGED MARRIAGES: JOINT/EXTENDED FAMILY, CULTURAL INJUNCTIONS, SEXUAL INHIBITIONS, DOWRY.

"We can't be sexually free with each other in a joint family... it is a problem for a good sex life."

"At our parents' home, we can't have sex."

Approximately half of the total respondents of this study think that joint family and extended family are an hindrance to sexual enjoyment and satisfaction. It is not the joint family or the extended family per se which is the problem, but it is the absence of privacy and the interfering mother-in-law and other relatives that seem to be disadvantageous for happy marital life. Although the majority of the respondents do not live in a joint family set up, in the traditional sense, nevertheless, many of them had one time or other had experienced coresiding with the extended family members. In spite of economic self sufficiency, many upper middle class and middle class couples choose to coreside with their parents or parents coreside with them, due to filial piety, filial obligations, economic consideration, emotional and physical needs.

It is also not uncommon for older relatives, and younger siblings or cousins to live with married couples. A single household is maintained to save on rent and to maximize economic benefit. Urban, educated, upper middle class and middle class couples have close connection, association or "jointness" with the extended family members. The rapid urbanization and modernization of India has not drastically changed the traditional family closeness.

Individuals who had lived in a joint family or with extended family members had their own bedrooms, but it is the close proximity of a married couples' bedroom to their in-laws' bedroom that causes sexual restraints. *"Even if we have our own bedrooms... privacy is still a problem"* is a recurring comment. Couples not having an attached bathroom to their bedroom were embarrassed and felt uneasy about using a common bathroom. There may not be a cultural prescription to wash or bathe before and after sexual intercourse, but Indian society is very fussy about personal cleanliness. A female school teacher, whose young brother-in-law was staying with her and her husband, complained how unmotivated she is about having sex with her husband. *"I feel very embarrassed to walk up to the common bathroom, because my brother-in-law sleeps in the living room."*

"Even if you have a separate bedroom, but if people are sleeping in the next room, certainly nobody likes to have sex." says a male field reporter.

"After my marriage, my unmarried sister-in-law was living with us... her bedroom was very close to our's... I was concerned about making noise... even if you have your own bedroom, your relatives are just outside your own bedroom" (a female radio transmission executive).

"We do have our own bedroom, even then it is a problem" is a common comment. Women, especially are afraid and embarrassed about their pleasure noises; a woman expressed how she holds all her bracelets, so that they do not make noise in the sexual acts. They are afraid about their beds squeaking. *"We have to make love when elders are away"*, says a male bank official. *"We have*

to sacrifice our pleasure for others... the joint family upsets and ruins the mood for sex", says a government officer.

"Soon after we came out of the joint family, we experienced orgasm... now it is like a whole universe merging...our bedroom was too close to my parents... sex was never satisfactory even up to ten years" a male program executive.

"Sex improved after getting out of the joint family" a male reporter.

What has orgasm got to do with living in a joint family system? A significant number of respondents expressed that they began to experience sexual pleasure and orgasm soon after they left their extended family structure. It is more than lack of privacy; living in a joint family or with members of extended family is an encroachment on the mental and emotional space of couples. These social constraints imposed on the married couples have an adverse effect on their experience of orgasm, puts a damper on motivation to have sex.

Couples' problem of inadequate privacy for intimacy seems to have long lasting repercussions on some of their children. A female sports director of an institution felt that her problems with sexual enjoyment is related to her witnessing her parents having sex. She commented, *"all of us used to sleep in the same room... many times I saw my parents having sex... I didn't like it... I think that is what influenced my negative attitude towards sex... that is why I have lost interest in sex."*

Nevertheless, inadequate privacy for sexual intimacy also has a counter argument; a male professor of Economics felt that watching his parents, and uncle and aunt making love liberated him from sexual inhibitions. *"When I was 7 years old, I saw my father making love to my mother... I have seen my uncle and aunt making love... we used to sleep in the same room. This developed positive attitude towards sex when I became an adult."* Another man, who rates his sex life as 7 on a scale of 1-10, says, *"one day we were making love, my father walked in on us."* He seems to be unflappable in spite of this incident.

An additional factor that plays a decisive role in couples' diminished enjoyment of sex is the mother-son's emotional attachment. Some men and women of this study reported that their sexual enjoyment is affected by their invasive mothers/mothers-in-law; they restrict and structure the time their daughters-in-law spend with their sons. A young, recently married microbiologist was displeased with his mother, a medical doctors for restricting his sexual enjoyment, spontaneity and frequency. He reported:

"After I got married, I took one month's leave just to enjoy sex... we used to make love 3-4 times during the day. My mother said, "you do what you want to do, but you should restrict yourself." Now, I can't have sex with my bride during the day."

"The bedroom should not be locked during the day time is the standing order of a mother-in-law. So, if couples want to make love during the day, they can't." (a female lecturer in botany).

"In a joint family, some mothers-in-law peep in on their son and daughter while they are in their bedroom." says a female media executive.

"My mother-in-law lives with us. She doesn't nag me, but in your mind you create your own barrier, because you are alert about her presence." (a female media official)

A recently married female physician reported that her widowed *"domineering"* mother-in-law restricts the privacy of the young bride with her new husband. *"My mother-in-law orders us to come out of our bedroom"* and insists that *"it makes me happy to watch T.V. with you and my son"..."she likes to tag along with us wherever we go."*

As already alluded to in the section on **Socialization** and in the section on the role of the mother in a man's selection of his marital partner, Indian mothers have a close bond and an warm emotional attachment to them. Kakar (1981:80-81) argues that the mother/infant son "physical closeness" results in "decisive, deep attachment to the nurturing mother." From the Kakar perspective, one can argue that mother's intervention into his son and daughter-in-law's intimate life may be due to mother's fear of losing her son– the "savior." Her expectations may provoke her to unconsciously demand "that the child serve as an object of her own unfulfilled desires and wishes, however antithetical they may be to his own" (Ibid, 88,89). Similarly, Kurtz (1992:103) in agreement with Kakar, states that 'the mother's frequent ministrations prompt a child to have a 'powerful emotional attachment to her". Obeyesekere (1990) findings also support the view that Indian men are still tied to mother's apron strings and show unfaltering devotion to them.

Such maternal indulgence may result in sexual jealousy between mother-in-law and daughter-in-law and competition for son's treasured love and loyalty. A mother-in-law may see her daughter-in-law as someone stealing the attention and affection that a son has bestowed upon her all these years. Mother-in-laws sexual jealousy of their daughter-in-laws comes from the latter replacing the former as "nurturer and most intimate partner of the son" states, Lamb (2000:75). Sometimes religious injunction is used to control the sex lives of couples; a male medical representative, commenting on the invasive, superstitious grandmothers, mothers and mothers-in-law said,

"During ashada (inauspicious season of the year), *sexual union is not recommended... they (older orthodox women) interfere into our sex lives and say, "it is bad to have sex during ashada."*

Procreational sex is fine, but not recreational! It was not uncommon to hear that couples find it difficult to display their affection and physical intimacy in the form of hugging and kissing their spouses in front of parents or in-laws. Sexual spontaneity or sexual flirtation is hindered; *Sexual urges don't come only in the night... it may come at any time, but you can't make love at your free will because of the constraints of the extended family."* (a male radio and television station officer).

"We would like to hug and kiss each other and act playful, but in a joint family, we have to watch ourselves" reported a female bank official. *"For intimacy to be developed, you have to be left alone... you can't show your affection to your husband... you have to watch yourself"* stated another woman.

"I am living in a joint family... it is difficult for sexual freedom... to express sexual intimacy. I can't watch T.V. sitting next to my husband... holding his hand, kiss him, especially in front of unmarried in-laws... there are restrictions... it (joint family) is inhibiting... whatever you do, you do in the constraints of your bedroom." (a female professor of physics).

Insensitivity on the part of the joint family members towards married couples' sexual needs is another common issue: *"in-laws and other relatives do not understand the importance of sex. It is very difficult to have privacy, even to hug and kiss"*, says a business woman. Although the elders would like to be assured that their sons and daughters marriage is a happy one, a spontaneous "public" display of affection may be seen as improper. Hinduism promotes pro-sex and life affirming attitudes; however, the people's behavior and attitudes do not necessarily reflect it. *"Indian society is sick and repressive,"* comments a male professor of English.

A married woman flaunting her sexuality is considered improper and damaging to her image because she is not acting as a 'mother' and a 'wife'. She is knocking herself off the pedestal. An ideal woman is one who shows sexual constraints in a joint family or with members of the extended family. Kakar (1989:17) analyzing Indian society's cultural attitudes towards women comments, a woman becomes a respected being, by assuming the roles of a wife, who performs prescribed Hindu rituals along with her husband and as a mother. Just as a woman, as a sexual being, she receives scorn. He further states, "there is a general disapproval of the erotic aspect of married life... {and there are} cultural injunctions that increase the conflicts around sexuality".

Scholars have reported, as noted earlier, that in a joint/extended family emotional and physical close ties between husbands and wives are discouraged in order to preserve the harmony and stability of the joint/extended family. Derné (1994) also reports that the preservation of harmony of the joint family was a reason for weak close ties between husbands and wives, the subjects of his study. Any overt display of affection or tenderness by the couple is a challenge to the balance of power and affection that exist in a joint or extended family, before a daughter-in-law or son-in-law enters it. A couple has to adjust themselves to the new alignment/realignment of roles-- father/father-in-law, mother/mother-in-law, sister/sister-in-law, brother/brother-in-law, uncle/aunt, grandfather/grandmother.

Furthermore, a couple displaying their affection in front of in-laws may be seen as a self-interested and insensitive act especially when there are unmarried in-laws or siblings in the same household. In a collectivistic society with the tradition of joint/extended family, couples are not expected to fulfill their needs of emotional intimacy and companionship exclusively with each other. Rather, they are expected to find the same also with other members of the joint family or extended family and forge strong bonds with them. A couple cozying up in the presence of others members may be seen as a threat to the cohesiveness and harmony of the larger family. Hence, it becomes difficult to balance marital identity and closeness with the demands and expectations of the extended family members. There is a fear of self-absorbed couples who may ignore the interests and needs of the other members. Parents fear that their son is being "henpecked".

Kakar (1981) suggests that an exclusive close intimate relationship of a couple within a joint family may create doubts in the family elders about loyalties. There are concerns about sons and daughters-in-law shirking the responsibility of their respective roles, if they shift their loyalties to each other. The ultimate responsibilities of a son and a daughter-in-law is to the joint family and their own interests are subservient to the larger family.

Sexual jealousies and sexual intrigues develop sometimes in a joint/ extended family. A male bank manager commented how, *"if a mother-in-law is young and attractive, a son-in-law may be attracted to her."* It is simply not the interfering mother-in-law, who is a problem. The physical and emotional proximity of individuals in an extended family leads to complications of relationships:

"There are sexually frustrated unmarried sisters, widows and divorcees that cause problems... they are kill joys... if my husband and I have a fight, my

unmarried sister-in-law was happy and lively" (a female professor).

"Sometimes my husband and I get up late on a Saturday morning... not only my mother-in-law gets very upset with us, but even my unmarried sister-in-law gets upset... she doesn't like us to take a nap in the afternoon" (a female bank official).

Mothers, mothers-in-law and other elderly female relatives interfere into couples' marital life and fertility decisions and put pressure on the newly married couple to start a family. Nagpal (2003:61), noting the power of middle-age Indian women states, "During middle age, she heads towards the identity of a powerful demi-matriarch with control over vital functions affecting the family...". Such control is pointed out by a subject of this study , a businessman: *"Elders inhibit our sex lives... we wanted to enjoy sex for 2-3 years before we have a child, but our elders put pressure on us to have a child soon."* Couples' fecundity should be validated within a year after marriage, otherwise relatives and friends begin to wag their tongues, asking oblique questions such as, *"has anything happened yet ?, "nothing has happened yet"!* And this is embarrassing to the young couples' parents. Success of a marriage and deep commitment to it are established by having a child, preferably a son. *"My mother-in-law was dead against us using contraceptives... my husband was very unhappy when I got pregnant... he even suggested an abortion,"* says a journalist. *"Elders insist on couples having a baby soon after the wedding... especially if they suspect marital problems... they want to tie you up to the marriage..."* says another female. A young newly married woman says, *"I don't want to have a baby soon, but my husband wants a baby... he doesn't want to use condoms because my mother-in-law is insisting that I should conceive in the next 6 months... there is no sexual understanding between my husband and me."* There is a strong belief that birth of a first child solidifies a marriage.

Motherhood is exalted in Indian society, while barren women are demoted in their status. In Hindu tradition, "woman" and "mother" are synonymous. It is through child bearing, especially bearing a son, that a woman achieves higher status, acceptance, respect and recognition from her husband's family. Parents are thrilled when their daughter/daughter-in-law bears a son. Now a husband can rest assured that his soul will achieve salvation as his son can light the funeral pyre. A well-defined self-identity is established now that she is a mother. Furthermore, as Kakar (1981) suggests motherhood, especially birth of a son, assures women more secure status. This is not only a cultural belief but also an observation shared by many scholars.

Even in upper middle and middle class educated families, university educated men and women still are expected to comply to the expectations of the elders of the family. Mothers and mothers-in-law try to exercise their will on their adult children and on sons-in-law, especially on daughters-in-law. It is all about power and control. The only power older women seem to have is the domestic power; control over their children and daughters-in-law. Living in a joint family could be a source of conflict and tension, especially for women, leading to marital discord and sexual dissatisfaction. Because of some domineering mothers-in-law, a daughter-in-law is wedged between her husband and her mother-in-law; the husband is torn between his mother and wife. He wants to please both the women, but ends up complying to his mother's wishes. *"You can always get another wife, but not another mother"* is a cultural statement that is made to show devotion to mothers.

Some women expressed their dissatisfaction with their mothers-in-law as they are expected to get "permission" from them for visits and trips. *"Even to go to my mother's, I should get permission from my mother-in-law... my husband says, I should obey her... he tries to mediate between her and me... I try to compromise... mother-in-law does not adjust to you... you have to adjust to her."* (a female bank officer). The interests of the larger family is more important than individuals' interests; filial respect and obedience, and compliance to the elders' expectations are seen as virtues.

Many Indian and Western sociologists have pointed out the stifling nature of the Indian caste system and the joint family arrangement. Although most respondents of this study acknowledge the benefits of the joint family as stated in the last chapter, nevertheless, they have experienced or have heard of others' unpleasant experiences. In the hierarchical structure of the joint family, the elders control the younger and middle aged family members. They are seen as choking the independence, individualism, initiative, spontaneity, and free will of the individuals-- a threat to personality development.

"Respect for one's privacy and understanding of the family members" are pointed out as important factors in avoiding marital unhappiness in a joint/ extended family. Individuals who live or lived in a joint family or extended family structure which respected their physical and mental space, and also had understanding and considerate family members, do not see that joint family is an hindrance to their marital satisfaction. *"My wife and I live with my parents.... It does not affect my intimate life. I have lot of privacy"* stated a male professor. Respondents who had no difficulties with the joint family commented about the benefits of living in such type of family arrangement. Women enjoyed an amicable relationship with their mothers-in-law.

Although most respondents think that the Hindu religion promotes a positive attitude towards sex, nevertheless, a considerable number of respondents think Indian society is an inhibited society. *"There is hypocrisy about sex, in fact, it is rare for a lady like you to talk about sex,"* says a male scientist. Men also feel that they were responsible for their brides' sex education, *"the mothers keep sex as a secret and do not educate their daughters... some brides do not allow their husbands to have intercourse with them even 6-8 months after the wedding"* noted a male professor of botany.

"Indian society is a repressed society... they are against girls and boys meeting and spending time together" notes an assistant general manager of a state radio station.

A small number of women brought up an interesting issue, that is, the ambiguous nature of men regarding their wives' sexuality. *"Men seem to have an ambiguous and rigid attitude about how women should perform in bed... good women are the wives and bad women are the ones who do interesting things in bed... never a combination of both..."* says a business woman. A media official says, he wants his wife to be a *"good wife,"* a *"good mother," but also have qualities of a prostitute in bed."* These contradictory expectations are seen by women as confusing.

Even after several years of marriage, uninhibited sex, meaning performing sex in complete nudity and with the lights on, continue to be a source of disagreement and conflict between husbands and wives. It is the men who were dissatisfied with their wives inhibited behavior, not vice versa. A male program executive who is married for more than 10 years says,

"Removing clothes is a big problem for my wife... she is improving slowly now... but inhibition is still there... she doesn't take much interest in foreplay...she is passive...she hates oral sex and different positions... sex is always on my mind... I have not been able to fulfill my sexual desire."

A male engineer, married for more than ten years, is satisfied with the diversity in his sex life with his wife, but he is still not pleased with his wife's certain inhibitions. *"We do different sexual positions... yes, we have oral sex. I enjoy love making in front of the mirror, but she doesn't like it... she likes the lights off."*

Why don't women like to perform sex with complete nudity and with lights on? It is more than sexual inhibition.

"The baby is sleeping next to me... I can't have the lights on" says a female lecturer. Another woman said, "when my husband approaches me sexually, I tell him I am tired... we have a 3-year-old child sleeping between us... when she is there I don't feel like having sex, we have to sleep in full clothes... we can't put the child in another room." Some women feel, "I don't have a gorgeous figure... I don't like to remove clothes and have lights blaring at me".

Another aspect of male complaint about inhibited wives is this; women feel if they express their sexual needs and desires, they may be seen as unfeminine. As a female engineer put it;

"I can't talk too freely with my husband about my sexual desires and his arousal skills... lest they (men) think we are too demanding, knowledgeable about sex... there is a fear that they suspect you might have had a sexual relationship before."

The present study did not deal with the issue of dowry and its effect on sexual behavior. There is no documentation of the male respondents who have received dowry or the female respondents who have given dowry to the men they married. Nevertheless, women did bring up on their own the issue of dowry and its effect on sexual interest and enjoyment. *"Dowry is a result of consumerism... imitating the West... people want to improve their economic standard."* They feel dowry is a social evil and a dehumanizing social practice, and most importantly, it has an adverse effect on the sexual relationship of couples.

"In an educated family, a girl gave her husband, an engineer, 4 laks of rupees as dowry... her in-laws always nagged her the whole day for not bringing a bigger dowry... and in the night they put pressure on her to have sex with her husband when she has no interest in him sexually... she is brooding the whole day because of in-laws nagging, then she goes through sex mechanically... her in-laws' bedroom is right next to the couples' bedroom... they are watching her behavior." (a female college professor)

"Women are not relaxed sexually if they are under pressure from the in-laws about the dowry" (a male Physics professor).

To conclude, the development of sexual attraction and satisfaction among arranged married couples is a gradual, slow process that demands commitment, patience and understanding from both the partners. As noted earlier, the majority of them were not sexually attracted on their first encounters, but a higher percentage of them developed some sexual attraction during the period of engagement before the marriage. Nevertheless, their sex life is fulfilling and satisfying. Even the couples who developed sexual attraction after the marriage catch up with the couples who were attracted to each other before marriage in sexual satisfaction with time. *Kala* (or time) is the best promoter of sexual attraction and satisfaction. So, marriage is a prerequisite for sexual attraction and gratification, not vice versa.

5

HOW DOES LOVE DEVELOP AFTER THE MARRIAGE ? OR IS LOVE MISSING IN ARRANGED MARRIAGE?

WHAT IS THE DEFINITION OF LOVE ? WHAT KIND OF LOVE DO THEY HAVE ?

"In love marriages, (romantic marriage) love begins before marriage. In arranged marriage, we begin to love each other after the marriage."

"I think once the marriage is settled, falling in love comes naturally... when you don't know the person it is only sexual attraction. It is only after marriage you fall in love." (female radio program coordinator)

"Love grows slowly... but the seeds were planted when I met him."

For many men and women of this study sexual fondness and love for each other developed after marriage as a result of similarities, the affable and compatible qualities of their mates, and as a result of respect and understanding that emerged after the marriage.

"Compatibility of factors helped in the development of love... love developed after the marriage because of similar values and principles," reports a male bank official.

"Love developed six months after the marriage because of his gentle nature, soft-spokeness, very understanding nature, rational and analytical qualities" reports a female bank official.

"Real love develops slowly, gradually."

"Living with him gradually developed love... started loving him as my husband."

"Love won't happen all of a sudden...after marriage... it was a gradual process... his patience, caring attracted me to him."

"Day by day after marriage, we began to love each other."

"Love comes only later, at the beginning it is only physical."

Love in arranged marriage is posterior to marriage and sex. With the exception of two respondents, nobody decided to marry because they loved their marital partner. Although a slightly larger number of the sample had developed some feelings of love during the engagement or acquaintance than individuals who had no feelings of love, for the majority of individuals, love evolved slowly after their marriage and after living with each other as husband and wife. Similarities play a decisive role. *"It is only after you get married...after coming to know the person, you fall in love... as the years progress..."* says a female media officer. Indians really know how to put the cart before the horse and also make it run rather smoothly !! Individuals condition themselves to fall in love with their marital partners which can be seen as a strategy for marriage survival. Fisher (2004:74) citing Aron and Aron; Aron et.al (1991,1995,1996) point out how the latter promote the idea that romantic love is not an emotion, but "a motivation system designed to enable suitors to build and maintain an intimate relationship with a preferred mating partner." Falling in love with a "preferred" mating partner with shared similarities and a commitment to maintain strong marital bond, then, act as a motivation system to develop feelings of love. As couples live their married life, they begin to experience "arranged love" as they say it.

In a small study conducted by Gupta and Singh (1982) in India, the researchers found that those couples whose marriages were based on love reported a decline in feelings of love and attraction after two to five years of marriage. Whereas, those couples in arranged marriages reported that their love and attachment had grown in the same period of time.

A male journalist quoted an Indian proverb, "lust produces love, love produces lust," to make a point about how love and sex are intertwined. He continued, *"both lust and love should be there together... if there is sexual satisfaction, it will generate love automatically... you can't separate them."*

It is the sexual intimacy between two strangers that gradually produces love, is the view of some respondents. *"Sex brings people closer... binds them together...then love develops. What holds the two together is sex."* A couple may have fights, but the Indian sexual wisdom tells, "couples fight until they make love" and "like a bee is attracted to honey, so does a man to a woman." Das (1993) also notes there is a cultural belief that sexual relation between spouses creates strong natural bonds between them.

Fisher (2004) in her discussion of relationship between lust and love states that studies indicate hormone of sexual desire can trigger feelings of love. The interconnectedness of lust and love are noted in this study. *"Love and sex are the same medium... they grow after a sexual relationship... arranged marriage brings couples together and arranges for them to have sexual relationship after marriage... their love relationship becomes stronger after the sexual union"* says a male professor of Economics. Such a notion was also noted among women subjects of this study. Similarly, Puri's (1999:120,121) analysis of her female narratives reveal the inextricable nature of sex and emotional love, but then she adds, "since sex is seen as instrumental to a more fulfilling emotional relationship with one's husband, without its emotional connection, sex would be seen as lacking in this framework." Although some men in this study may see *"sex and love are the same medium,"* one cannot establish whether they see lack of emotional bond with their wives (if there is) would affect their sex lives in the way it may affect women who may have weak emotional bonds with their husbands.

Love in an arranged marriage evolves slowly in a continuum:

Assessment Stage:

"We liked each other when we met... same caste, language, we like

music and literature... come from the same class background... both of us are university educated and professionals."

When two suitable, potential marriage partners are arranged to meet, they assess the social-economic and intellectual similarities and compatibility of each other with the assistance of their parents or family elders. Similarity of values and beliefs are also stressed. At this stage, if there is a suspicion of any physical deformities of the suitors or family health history, or family reputation, or the character of the potential suitors (especially women's character), the wedding proposal is withdrawn. Any doubts about the dissimilarities of socio-cultural or economic factors that may have the probability of marital maladjustment also result in termination of the wedding proposal.

Commitment to Commit Stage:

"After a few times meeting, we decided to marry... we had everything going for us."

Now that the best possible deal is done, the future marital partners accept each other and commit themselves to marry without knowing each other very well.

Acquaintance Stage:

"We talked about our future... the children, our obligations to the parents and in-laws;" "I told her about my income... she has to adjust;" "I liked his nature... caring, understanding personality."

After the commitment to marry is completed, couples try to get to know each other; their financial status, their interests, their obligations to and involvement in the extended family, personality, and habits. More importantly, they begin to understand the mutual role expectations of each other as a married couple. At this stage, couples may get engaged.

Attraction stage:

"We are very much alike in many aspects... it is like a mental shorthand... it become easy to get attracted and fall in love"

Similarities play role in mutual attraction-people are attracted to people like themselves. *"He and I are so compatible with each other... I began to fall in love with him"* says an artist. *"I feel so comfortable with him"; "When I am with her I don't have to explain anything"* – an indescribable feeling of lightness, comfort and closeness that motivates people to like or love each other. Now, they are emotionally connecting.

"We began to like each other... but no sexual attraction or love." "We began to be sexually attracted to each other...some feelings of love were there."

"We did everything except sex."

Couples begin to cultivate feelings of love and physical attraction during the period of engagement, but for some, it is a stage of just beginning to feel comfortable with each other. Those who feel sexually attracted to each to other, may begin to become sexually intimate; kissing, caressing and fondling, but in most cases, the consummation is reserved strictly to the ritualistic 'first night'.

Committed stage:

Men and women condition themselves to fall in love with each other, because they are committed to each other. *"Once you get married, you must learn to respect and love each other and have commitment for each other"* is what young people hear as part of their socialization.

"We made a commitment to each other on our wedding day–commitment that is indissolvable."

This stage begins with the wedding day–a day of promise to stay committed to each other and to remain lifelong marital partners. As noted earlier, the couples are asked to perform a holy ritual called *satyapadi* and recite a prayer from the *Rigveda*; *"Don't give up my sakha (partner). Let us will to be united."*

Companionate Love Stage:

"Love took some time to start... over the years she stood by me through

my financial problems... she is a selfless person" (an English professor).

"My husband is a considerate, caring, thoughtful man.. a good man."

Now that they are man and wife, and their lives are deeply intertwined, sharing joys and sorrows, companionate love begins to bloom. It is a less intense love based on commitment, care, long enduring affection, consideration, mutual respect and *dharma* (duty).

Attachment-Reconciled Stage:

Companionate love leads to adjustment to each other's needs and weaknesses and attachment to and dependency on each other in spite of marital conflicts and some marital ups and downs. Attachment is that nice feeling of being totally accustomed to each other, characterized by unconditional mutual acceptance, and tolerance of mutual weakness. Shared similarities create feelings of comfort and closeness.

Couples may not say *"I love you"* to each other as we hear often in the western culture, but there is an inexplicable affection, silent and strong, but not intense. During this stage, there is an unique style of communication; *"We talk a lot to each other," "we don't talk to each other much."* Silence itself becomes a vehicle of communication for some. Mutual dependency grows with time leading to a sense of well-being, marital stability and security. As Liebowitz (1983) theorizes, the attachment stage of love produces endorphins in partners that create some of the aforementioned feelings. Fisher (2004:89) also proposes that "cuddle chemicals," such as vasopressin and oxytocin contribute to feelings of closeness and attachment with one's partner.

What is this thing called love ?

What the definitions of love and the behavior and attitude of marital lives of the respondents suggest is that they seem to have a stable, secure, strong, committed, comfortable marital life with quiet, enduring affection-features of *companionate love, as stated by Tennov (1980).* It is a deep, affectionate attachment, "the affection we feel for those with whom our lives are deeply intertwined" as Myers (1993:494) puts it. This companionate love may be a factor in their reporting marital satisfaction and contentment in marital life.

The word "love" has different meanings to different individuals. So much so, nearly 30 different definitions of love are revealed in this study:

Love is defined as: *"sharing of the good and the bad," "cooperation," "devotion," "commitment," "care," "respect," "patience," "unconditional," "accepting the other person as he/she is," "sharing of mind," "mutual acceptance," "compromise," "duty," "mutual freedom," "compromise," "trust," "100% freedom," "not commanding," "not demanding," "consideration," "understanding," "harmonious relationship," "mutual happiness," "mutual responsibility," "friendship," "to do what pleases her/him," "unselfishness," "love is not sex," "love is sexual," "love is not thinking about any other person other than the one you are married to."*

Several striking features emerge out of the innumerable definitions of love; they are not self-centered and self-serving definitions, rather they are centered around their spouses well-being and satisfaction. In addition, the definition of love is relational that includes reference to "we," rather than "I." The "we" concept is consistent with the Hindu belief of "*ardhangi*" (the other half), which states that human beings were divided by gods long ago and they are seeking their other half when they seek a marital partner. So, love is seen as a fusion and blurring of identities. Hence, the purpose of marriage is not for self-actualization, but it is in a way, you become complete with your other half: in that sense it is self-actualization. Very few had reference to the sexual or the passionate aspect of love. The relational model of couples may fit into the model of commitment as primary, and love and sex are of secondary consequence or subordinated to commitment.

Lastly, unlike in western societies where people separate issues of love, sex, commitment, marriage; in the respondents definition of love, all the aforementioned components of relationship are seen as a mono-ideology or encompassing. That is, in western societies you may have casual fun sexual relationship based on sexual attraction without loving that person or having commitment or marriage plans. But in Indian society, generally speaking love, sex, commitment and marriage appear to be interconnected and inseparable.

Although major differences in definition of love were not noted between male and female respondents, female respondents' ideology of love reveal self-sacrifice. *"To do what pleases him," "dharma," "duty," "devotion"* are perceived as the definitions of love among some women. This love ideology is consistent with the cultural ideology of how women should define love. Interestingly Derné 's study on men, which did not include only university educated professionals as this study, revealed that their definition of love "is based on duty owed in a relationship, not on special qualities of the beloved individual" (1995:74). Above mentioned definitions of love in this study showed that it included reference to the expected qualities and special qualities in a marital partner.

Based on the definitions of love and the description of respondents marriage, marital love in an arranged marriage is a combination of "agape", "pragma" and "storge". Lee (1973) defines agape lovers as selfless or altruistic lovers; pragma as practical lovers who choose their mates based on socio-economic similarities; storge love as a slow developing love, but it is secure and trusting. It is based on friendship, companionship and shared interests. Storge lovers seek partners with similar values, and their relationship is rather unexciting and uneventful.

Women respondents' definition of love as *"devotion," "dharma," "self sacrificing," "unselfish," "unconditional"* suggest their marital love is characterized by agape love. This is consistent with the concept of an "ideal" Indian woman-- self-sacrificing, devoted wife who is called "pathivratha". The love ideology of self-sacrifice is ingrained into female consciousness during their socialization. As wives and mothers, they are expected to subordinate their needs, interests, autonomy, individuality, and happiness to their husbands and children. Even for professional women, their lives revolve around their husbands and children.

Sternberg (1986), taking solely a western perspective, argues for love to be complete, all three components of love-- passion, intimacy, and commitment must be present. Commitment without passion or love is empty love. He also sees companionate love as incomplete, as it does not have the "passionate" component. Passion, based on sexual love as a deciding factor for marriage, is seen as dubious in Indian society; it is believed passion wanes away and is not a good corner stone for a strong marriage. It is the commitment to brave all marital challenges that is considered important.

Although respondents report the presence of intimacy–feelings of closeness, connectedness, and emotional support that evolve gradually and slowly, it is the strong glue of commitment that is given ultimate priority in a marriage. Moreover, emotional intimacy is shared with the other members of extended family, not focused only on spouse and children. When the respondents were asked about their emotional intimacy with their spouses, there was less concern about it. They did not express a tremendous need to be emotionally intimate with their spouses, suggesting less of emotional nucleation. In a collectivistic society such as Indian society, emotional intimacy only with one's spouse is seen as self-interest, autonomous behavior. Well-being and marital satisfaction do not necessarily rest entirely on emotional intimacy with a spouse. Nor is it the basis for marriage.

Love within an arranged marriage is also reciprocal love. Analysis of the individuals' responses reveal that their love evolved gradually in a reciprocal manner after the marriage due to (a) similarities and compatibility- *"we began to love each other because we are so much alike... we have similar desirable characteristics"; (b)* mutual appreciation and mutual need satisfaction–*"my husband is thoughtful, kind and understanding; "my husband makes sure I enjoy myself (sexually)... he waits until I come"* (c) mutual expression of affection and love, care and understanding– *"my husband loves me and cares for me... I also love and care for him in return;" "She began to love me... and I also began to love her gradually."* Love grows as reflexive and reinforcing behavior.

Couples begin to cultivate and condition reciprocal love for each other after their marriage. It is what some people call "arranged love." Feelings of love and sexual attraction generate cycle of love and sexual attraction. They create the *feeling* that they love each other and find each other sexually attracted to each other. They begin to believe it is so. And in time, it becomes a self-fulfilling prophecy, escalating their feelings for each other, but it may not be intense. As Aronson (1998) puts it "merely believing someone likes you can initiate a spiraling series of events that promote increasingly positive feelings between you and the other person."

6

HOW AND WHY ARRANGED MARRIAGES LAST? WHAT MAKES A GOOD MARRIAGE? DO INDIVIDUALS HAVE REGRETS ABOUT THEIR ARRANGED MARRIAGE?

"If I were to do it all over again, I would prefer arranged marriage, because love marriages are failures... they exhaust each other and see their mutual differences later. I prefer arranged marriage, because of stability, better understanding, compatibility, family's moral support in times of crisis" (a male professor of Botany).

"In spite of my average sex life, I consider my marriage as successful... I am definitely happy... if I were to do it all over again, I'll go through arranged marriage... I don't find any weakness in arranged marriage" (a female athletics director).

"If I were to do it all over again, I don't think I'll love first and marry, I'll marry, then I'll love" (a female professor).

"I prefer arranged marriage... love marriage is risky because you don't know the family... I like the choice within arranged marriage" (a female program executive).

"I wanted to select a girl of my choice and my taste without the intervention of my parents... luckily for me everything has gone on smoothly in our marriage... no regrets about my arranged marriage" (a transportation executive).

"All the factors are compatible in our marriage, including there is sexual compatibility, even tho' I didn't know her sexually... no regrets about arranged marriage" (a businessman).

"In arranged marriage we trust" seems to be the cultural belief. Respondents of this study were asked, "if you had to do it all over again, would you prefer to have an arranged marriage, or would you prefer to fall in love and marry?" A considerable majority of them felt that they would prefer to have an arranged marriage, if they were to do it all over again. They also expressed they have **no** regrets about their arranged marriage and would marry the **same** man or the woman they are married to now. As indicated earlier, the attitude of **reconciliation without renunciation** of traditional values is a striking feature of these subjects. Chand's (1989) study adds an interesting point; the marital success of her subjects in India did not depend on the type of marriage, whether it is an arranged marriage or "love" marriage (marriage by choice). Rather, it depended ultimately on the adjustment the marital partners made with each other.

It may be recalled that the **Before Marriage Group** reported presence of sexual attraction before the marriage, positive "first night" experience and higher sexual satisfaction than the **After Marriage Group.** Nevertheless, the majority of the total respondents feel that they have a "good marriage" and they think they have marital satisfaction. So, what factors are responsible for their good marriage ? But, first, what is a "good marriage"?

Most people define a "good marriage" as one in which both the partners have *"dharma"* (duty or moral obligation) *towards each other," "dharma towards children and to the extended family;" "love, care and deep commitment," "satisfying sex lives;" "respect and tolerance of each other and the extended family members;" "good understanding;" "compromise and flexibility."* In spite of the fact that the respondents of this study are university educated professional people, they feel men and women adhering to their traditional gender roles contribute to a good marriage. But, their definition of traditional gender role does not restrict women from paid employment. Rather, it refers to the traditional role professional women are expected to play in their domestic role and in their interactions with their husbands and children.

Why do arranged marriages work ? Individuals consider the following factors as responsible for marital satisfaction and a good marriage. These factors are also seen as the strengths of arranged marriage.

Extended Family Support:

"When a brick in a water tank begins to break, you must immediately fix it, othe, wise the whole water tank will break down... this is how the family elders help us in holding the marriage together" (a male media official).

The majority of the respondents feel that the extended family's emotional, moral, and financial support play an important role in their experiencing good marriage. Most people share the same thoughts and opinions regarding the strengths of arranged marriage and the beneficial role of the extended family in their marriage:

> *"An arranged marriage lasts long because it is based on the judgment of the entire family... there is stability and security in marriage and family. Even if there are marital problems, the family elders tackle the problem... they advise us by saying you should tolerate each other...understand each other... life is both pain and pleasure... "*
>
> *"The family gives stability and support our marriage."*
>
> *"The experience and wisdom of our elderly are of great help in our marriage."*
>
> *"Both our families provide moral support and financial security."*
>
> *"There is a better understanding between husbands and wives because of the elders good decision"* (about selection of a marital partner).

A feature of collectivistic society, as mentioned earlier, is this--couples maintain a close relationship with their parents and other extended family members who provide economic support and emotional intimacy for their personal well-being. This may lead to less psychological intimacy and emotional nucleation between husband and wife, but the benefit may be in reduced marital strain. Marriage is not seen as a path to fulfill one's various psychological needs–"*it is not a marriage in which there are three people that is, me, myself and I.*" Couples also spend less time with each other, as they are involved in multifarious "quid pro quo" social and economic activities and commitments related to extended family and friends. Involvement in socially integrative activities with other family members and friends give couples their own mental and physical space--an asset for marital satisfaction and makes less demand on the nuclear family. The Japanese have an interesting expression called "living together loneliness"–a result of long married life. While it may be true of many marriages with long marital duration, the involvement in the extended family responsibilities and activities vastly reduces this "living together loneliness."

It is interesting to note here that Wallerstein and Blakeslee, in their book *The Good Marriage* (1995), argue the first task in any marriage is to separate psychologically from the emotional ties of the family of origin. Furthermore, they contend marriages fail because couples are unable to separate from the original family. In Indian society severing emotional ties from the original family would be considered disastrous to the stability of marriage. As people see it, it is the extended family that gives stability to the marriage. "*The extended family helps us to cope with marital stress.*"

Individuals are under the supervision and social control of their extended families who expect the couples to make their marriage work and to "*hold the samsara together*" (*samsara* means family, both the nuclear and extended family, but its literal translation from Sanskrit means, "that which flows together"). Family members are expected to stick together through their entire lives, not disrupting its cohesiveness. As soon as the young couples get married they are reminded by the family elders, "*Now you have to act married,*" meaning they have to assume marriage and Hindu ritual responsibilities and all the role expectations that are associated with the status of being married. Extended family members play a key role in fortifying marital commitment;

"Arranged marriage is binding, because so many family members are involved in the marriage decision... the family stands by you."

As many respondents recognized, *"One strength of arranged marriage is the family support in all respects. Couples are under pressure to make the marriage work, because of family status and prestige;" "also parents have made so much of effort in finding the right partner."* A failed marriage is an embarrassment to the parents.

As parents are involved in the selection of a suitable partner, individuals feel free to discuss marital problems with them and look to them for guidance at times of marital discord. *"In a love marriage, we have conflicts with parents; such problems are not there in an arranged marriage, and we can freely discuss marital problems with them,"* says a businessman. Whereas, if marital conflicts emerge in love (romantic) marriages, parents are likely to remind the couples, *"we told you so."* In a love marriage, *"you take responsibility for yourself." "You become isolated from your family members."* But on the other hand, people who opted for arranged marriage feel, if they have marital problems they are not entirely responsible for it, rather the parents and relatives who arranged the marriage have to take the blame.

There is a certain confidence that extended family will support couples at times of misfortune or tragedies or serious marital difficulties. They are seen as marriage counselors, conflict arbitrators, and as an unifying force:

> *"In case your spouse dies, you can return to your family... they will take care of you and the children."*
>
> *"If we have any problems, parents will stand by us..."*
>
> *"Moral support of both of the families is given during difficult times... also you can go back to your family (parents) in case of severe marital problems."*
>
> *"The elders resolve the marital conflicts."*

The extended family members are also of great help to professional women, who are dealing with the stress and conflict of juggling family with their profession. Child care centers are not easily acceptable, hence, it is the retired and stay-home older women who take care of the young and older children while their parents are at work. They feed them, tutor them, guide them and also act as transmitters of cultural values; thus contributing to the cohesiveness of the family. A male bank officer pointed out the advantages of living with the extended family; *"It is best to live with the extended family, because of cooperation of work, their advice, help... problems are solved with group effort."*

SOCIO-CULTURAL SIMILARITIES:

"I am very satisfied with arranged marriage... we are on the same frequency of thinking... I have never felt this kind of feeling with anyone, as I have felt with my husband."

"You should get married to a person like yourself... similarity is a tie that binds you... leading to good marital understanding... compatibility helps the marriage... gives stability, continuity..."

Marital compatibility, adjustment, and communication are less challenging if two individuals come from similar socio-cultural background. A female Economics professor is rather confident that it is the similarities of couples and knowledge of family background that gives the assurance that a *"marriage will work out 99%...* But she adds, *"you still have to make a lot of adjustment."* But individuals also recognize, *"in arranged marriage, there is a greater need for adjustment, because we are strangers to each other."*

Social-cultural similarities of marital partners account for the marital satisfaction, is the consensus of the respondents. Long before scholars such as Buss (1985), who pointed out the importance of socio-cultural similarities to marital satisfaction, and Lumpert (1997), who argued the greater the genetic similarity between marital partners, the greater their marital harmony and satisfaction, the ancient system of arranged marriage seem to have had a sharp insight into marital satisfaction. Chand's (1989) study seems to indicate a correlation between higher level of education and higher level of martial satisfaction among her subjects in India.

COMMITMENT AND TRUST

"Marriage is the reason for marriage."

"In an arranged marriage, the mind set is such, we would make the marriage work... we try to make the best of the situation... dissolving a marriage is a drastic step. You are married... whatever the odds, you try to put up with it... unless there is physical violence or ill treatment."

"If the marriage is not working, you work at it... you don't give up."

Hinduism considers marriage as sacred, an eternal and an indestructible union. It is one's *dharma* (moral duty or social responsibility) to have unfailing commitment to his/her marital partner. Remember the marriage vow, *nathicharami* (I won't leave you or violate you). These cultural injunctions not only give stability and continuity to marriage, but also provide marital satisfaction. Married couples are less anxious about whether their marriage will work or not. There is a feeling of complete security and trust which comes from tenacious commitment that helps in resolving marital problems and enduring marital crisis. Commenting on the good marriage, individuals recognize that *"commitment, trust, faith, and love"* as essential attributes. Couples are not only committed to each other, but also to the most enduring institution--marriage. In a study conducted by Yelsma and Athapilly (1988), it is noted that marital satisfaction in Indian arranged marriages may be related to life-long commitment and cultural tradition.

Individuals who opt for arranged marriage have made a leap of faith. They may be anxious about the unfamiliarity of their partners, but deep within them they trust the centuries old custom and in the sound judgment of their parents and in the consensus of older relatives. Shared similarities give them the confidence that the marriage will work. They are also very well aware of the fact that they have the ultimate burden to make the marriage work. Or else it may lead to divorce or separation, a consequence people would like to avoid to protect themselves from social stigma and demotion of social status. "Family breakers" are frowned upon. Cultural constraints of divorce motivate couples to make their marriage work.

In addition, relatively speaking compared to western societies there are less choices in Indian society not only in health care, financial investments, phone companies, and life opportunities, but also in relationships. Living in a "no choice" society (meaning a society that discourages choice about divorce or marital dissolution) may itself encourage marital satisfaction and stability. Barry Schwartz in his book, "The Paradox of Choice: Why More Is Less" discussing the burden of choice, argues that in American society, "increased choice can lead to decrease in satisfaction... there may be a point when choice tyrannizes people more than it liberates" (The New York Times, January 22, 2004).

Inherent in the Indian psyche is the idea that a marriage should not be dissolved, rather problems should be solved in an amicable manner without destabilizing the family and hurting the children. Relationships are not seen as casual and contractual. It is like someone commented, marriages should also follow the same policy as stores follow. "Goods once sold cannot be returned or exchanged" is a warning that is printed on merchandise receipts in India.

In cases when the marriage is not successful or happy, majority of couples decide to stay on in the marriage, because they got attached to or have reconciled with each other or because the well being of their children is more important than their own. *"It is my dharma* (moral duty) *to stay with her/him and not cause hurt to our children."* Acceptance and adjustment are seen as marital strategies. Even irreconcilable differences are reconciled and seen as complementary in nature, thus creating mutual dependency. In case the marriage is a total failure, they try to cope with stoic acceptance-*"it is my karma"*. Couples with very serious marital difficulties may choose to divorce, but may also decide to seek separation and live with their parents or relatives or alone. They maintain a phantom of marriage for society's sake.

A female real estate agent, who has separated herself from her husband because of irreconcilable differences, lives with her mother and maintains a congenial relationship with her husband. She cooks and packs food on a daily basis for her husband. *"There is no need for a divorce... I like this arrangement."* Not solving a marital problem is in itself a solution. Living with marital problems is less disruptive than resolving it. *"You don't have to cut the tree that is blocking your path, just get around it."*

Realistic/Low Expectations

"To expect perfection of your husband or wife is totally unrealistic" (a female professor).

"I am a person of ordinary endowment in all respects. So I expect my wife to be neither below nor above me" (a male scientist).

"My wife is short, plump... she is not a beauty... she doesn't share my literary interests... intrinsically, she is a good person... I respect her" (CEO of Radio and T.V. station).

A wedding ceremony is referred to as a "function" in Indian society. Perhaps this suggests the realistic, pragmatic view of marriage. It is said that the French have "happy" marriages, the Americans have happy divorces. But the Indians have marriage. The idea it is better to be married than not to be married is highly promoted. Before young couples marry parents, grandparents, and older relatives remind them, that *"marriage is not a bed of roses! "If a marriage has no problems... it is not a marriage... it is a fake marriage."* They condition them to lower their expectations of their marital partners and stress the importance of *"adjustment." "Somehow adjust yourselves to each other and go on for the sake of the children"* is a common advice. The word "adjust" has several meanings: it means one should adapt oneself to new circumstances, a new husband/new wife, new invasive in-laws, a nagging and controlling mother-in-law. It also means *"put up with or tolerate inconveniences," or "put up with the weakness of your husband/wife."*

"Adjust" also means acceptance and reconciliation of each other's weakness, foibles and idiosyncrasies. Another word of advice that is commonly used is; *"have contentment;"* meaning *"don't go after that elusive thing called happiness!"* Individuals desire marital contentment-- a satisfaction with what they **have,** rather than pursuing that indefinable, fleeting and unattainable feeling of eternal happiness.

As people have realistic and low expectations of their marital partner and marriage, this may contribute to marital satisfaction. When the expectations are high and unrealistic, the disappointment of not achieving them is greater than when you have low realistic expectations. This leads to what Diener (2000:40) calls "aspiration gap," leading to discontentment. As it may be recalled when respondents were asked about their "ideal" husband and wife, the majority of women stressed the importance of education, economic capability, family background, and pleasing personality traits. Men, on the other hand, stressed the importance of education and physical attractiveness, good family background, and of being a good mother and wife. There was no mention of unrealistic or unimportant expectations of each other, such as personal interests, hobbies, political or social views. These are not considered immensely important for the success of a marriage. To a certain extent, American marriages are more demanding and challenging for couples than marriages in India, as marital partners are not expected to satisfy **all** emotional, physical, intellectual, and interest needs.

A basic tenet of Hindu philosophy, based on the teachings of Lord Krishna in *Bhagavad Gita,* is the acceptance of "pleasure and pain with equal tranquility." These cultural values are likely to influence one's realistic expectations of marriage. Marriage is not a perfect bliss–it has both pleasure and pain. In fact, there is a festival of Hindu New Year, where it is a custom to eat a terribly bitter gourd along with sugar to remind people that life has both "bitterness and sweetness." There is also an ingrained belief and stoic acceptance of "nothing remains the same." So, married couples are culturally conditioned to expect marital problems, changes, different stages, and ups and downs with fortitude. They are asked *"somehow"* to find contentment and compromise in the present situation they are in; marital perseverance is a cultural value.

Tolerance, patience, compromise, and stoic acceptance of each other are considered as virtues necessary for marital satisfaction. *"We compromise a lot... this is what I have, so I might as well accept it."* It is believed a person who is not tolerant of human weakness becomes over-critical; such person is seen as one *"who tries to find sand in curds"* (yogurt). This adage refers to people who are so over-critical of others that they are capable of finding "sand" in yogurt. (It is believed that yogurt is pure, perfect sacred cow milk product- how could you find any impurity in it?)

Companionate Love/Collective Interest:

In romantic marriages, love is the reason for marriage, whereas in arranged marriages, marriage is the reason for love. It is the marriage that sustains love, and is not love that sustains the marriage. It may be recalled, the love ideology of the respondents have features of companionate love that develops within conjugal relationship. How one defines love may itself contribute to good marriage. Companionate love is even-tempered, stable, and strong; it is anchored in close monogamous relationship, commitment, and enduring affection. *"Once young people get married and start living together as husband and wife,* ***somehow*** *love will develop"* is the basic faith in marriage.

Companionate love is not a roller-coaster emotion as romantic love may be, but it develops slowly resulting in less fragile relationships and less emotional ups and downs. While there may not be passion or intense emotional longing for each other in companionate love, there is strong attachment, affection, and respect for each other. A conjugal-companionate love is rational; it is slowly and deliberately cultivated affection fraught with care and respect for the survival and welfare of the family. Couples do not find it necessary to assure each other by saying often, "I love you," as western couples often repeat to reinforce their love for each other. Trust in each other gives companionate couples a feeling of marital security, so much so, a verbal expression of "I love you," appears odd and awkward. A woman who was married to her husband for a long time was shocked that her husband one day called her from another town to say, *"I love you."* She got concerned about this "bizarre" behavior and asked him, *"are you o.k.? are you drinking a bit too much?"*

One thing that stands out in the respondents' definition of love is, as indicated earlier, it is not self-centered or based on individualism or self-autonomy. Rather, love is self-sacrificing, "we" oriented, and relational. *"Love is sacred... something an individual gives by sacrifice... it is a giving without holding back* state." What you can do to the family's happiness is more important than what the family can do for you. In *Bhagavad Gita,* Lord Krishna says *"man must free himself from the delusion of "I" and "mine."* This cultural injunction appears to be inculcated in the Indian psyche. As mentioned previously, love as experienced in an arranged marriage is a combination of "agape," "pragma," and "storge."

All these aspects of love ideology, in addition to seeing marriage not as a vehicle for self-actualization and self-fulfillment, may lead to a fulfilling marriage. Marriage is not meant to be customized for individual's interests and happiness. Unlike individualistic societies that stress individuals' happiness as an inalienable right, there is less preoccupation, less pressure to pursue the goal of personal happiness in Indian society. It may be reminded here that Hinduism sees marriage as an ideal, a family duty and social responsibility. In addition, in relational-based collectivistic societies, individuals are expected to sacrifice their individual happiness, self-interest and self-autonomy to the well-being of their nuclear and extended families. Such states "personal happiness occupies a less salient position in Eastern cultures than Western cultures and the Eastern cultures expect their societal members to subordinate their personal desires, goals, and aspirations to those of the collective" (2000:76). Maintaining a harmonious relationship with both their nuclear and extended families seems to contribute to their marital and life satisfaction. "If my husband/wife, children and parents are happy, I am happy" is a common definition of marital happiness in this study. Wallerstein & Blakeslee's (1995) study on factors related to good marriage in American society revealed similar aspect as in this study. They argue that a second task for a good marriage is not to focus on "me," but"... to expand the sense of self to include the other, while each individual carves out an area of autonomy. The overarching identification with the other provides the basis for bonding" (1995:331).

Collectivistic societies such as Indian society appear to contribute to marital satisfaction and a general well-being in another sense. Couples do not heavily depend solely on each other for their marital happiness and well-being. Rather their definition of marital satisfaction or general well-being is more "outer directed" than "inner directed." One's happiness is derived from close interpersonal relationships or it is connected to happiness of other family members, both nuclear and extended family members, who provide social and emotional support. There is some evidence from Sinha and Verma's findings (1994) that allocentrism was correlated with psychological well-being when mediated by high social support.

In discussing culture and subjective well-being, Kitayama and Markus (2000) suggest that individuals define subjective well-being differently across cultures and their definition is constructed by each society's social norms. They think unlike individualistic western societies, in collectivistic societies, a person's quality of life is defined collaboratively with others, rather than from an internal frame of reference. While it may sound that individuals, especially women, are sacrificing their self identity and their own happiness in a collectivistic society, it may be in their self-interest to find happiness in the larger group context by collaborating with other group members. As indicated earlier, Mines (1994:189,192) thinks "individuality finds expression within the context of social group, including family... "individuals need their relationships (with a group) in order to accomplish their own private ends. This requires them to nurture relationships that they consider important to their private interests."

Kitayama and Markus's (2000) study on Japan, a collectivistic traditional society as India, has also shown that good feelings and well-being of individuals are anchored in the cultural ideas of sympathy, compassion, mutual adjustment, sympathy, care, and help to others. In another closely related research finding, Suh (2000) found that in collectivistic cultures, individuals are more directed by societal norms and social appraisals in assessing their subjective well-being, than in individualistic societies where individuals are likely to use their internal frame of reference linked to one's own happiness in defining their well-being.

Although professional men and women of this study made their own choice regarding their marital partners, and they felt they had veto power regarding their choice, but yet, they married their marital partners that were arranged by their parents and promoted by them. One reason for their marital satisfaction may be they have acquiesced to their parents' expectations and desires--*"I am glad I married my parents' choice."* A support to this view is found in several studies: Markus and Kitayama (1991, 1994) and Radhakrishnan and Chan (1997). Markus and Kitayama think that individuals in collectivist cultures internalize family's expectations and their compliance with cultural norms seems to play a crucial role in their life satisfaction. The researchers further state that collectivist individuals' definition of good feeling is associated with cooperation and responsibility for group or family members, fulfillment of family members' obligations and expectations, and more than anything else, engaging in behaviors that are congruent with cultural norms. Radhakrishnan and Chan, in their comparison of American and Indian cultures, suggest that in collectivistic societies, living a life close to external standards, such as fulfilling parents' expectations and goals, is a good indicator of their life satisfaction. Suh and Diener's research (1999) further strengthens the argument that in collectivist societies parental approval and conformity to their expectations is a strong source of subjective well-being.

Sexual Satisfaction:

Despite the fact that the majority of the respondents were not sexually attracted to their spouses when they met each other for the first few times, an impressive majority of the total respondents reported moderate to high sexual satisfaction in their marriage. Nevertheless, the **Before Marriage Group** reported higher sexual satisfaction (due to sexual attraction) than the **After Marriage Group.** Sexual satisfaction and compatibility seem to strengthen marriages, in spite of some marital difficulties. A male engineer's view represents the views of other people:

"If we have sexual compatibility... we can overcome anything... we used to have fights before... but now they are reduced, because we are very compatible sexually... it has made our marriage stronger..."

Even though marital sexual satisfaction is important for a majority of the respondents, they are unlikely to dissolve a marriage because of sexual incompatibilities or inadequate sexual satisfaction. They felt:

"I am very satisfied with my sex life... but even if I am not satisfied... I'll not leave my husband."

"My sex life is terrible... she is frigid... but I'll not leave her for another woman."

"Absolutely no... even though she has not fulfilled all my sexual expectations... her sex drive is low."

"We would have not gotten out of marriage... if there was sexual incompatibility or less sexual satisfaction... we would have managed... marriage is a social responsibility...we have a son."

Hinduism considers *rati* (sexual pleasure) as an important third component of marriage, but yet, sexual pleasure does not dominate the importance of *dharma* (moral duty) and *praja* (progeny). A fine balance among the three components of marriage may facilitate a good marriage. *"If sexual satisfaction is the only criterion for a good marriage... it (marriage) might not work... but other things are important in a marriage"*, stated respondents. A harmony among the worldly attainments, *dharma, artha* (wealth), *kama* (love, desire) is the ultimate pursuit of Hindu religion.

Only 10% of the respondents reported having affairs because of sexual dissatisfaction or higher sexual need.

"I am sexually happy with my wife, but I have more sex drive than her... I need a longer foreplay, but she wants only sexual intercourse...she

wants it longer, but I climax. I have a lover... she and I have sex 3-4 times when we meet in a hotel once or twice a month" (a professor).

"My sexual urges are very high... my wife has incontinence... it disgusted me... I talked to my wife and parents about this problem. They protested the idea of my having two wives. I know it is illegal to have two wives in India... (for the Hindus) *but, I went through a Hindu ritual. Both of them live in the same house... one upstairs and another downstairs. I have two kids from the first wife and one kid from the second wife. My second wife is very attractive.... I make love to her 5 times a week and 2 times a week to my first wife, in spite of her incontinence. I love my first wife... the way she treats me... her cooking. My second wife is more attractive and sexier than my first wife... she satisfies me more sexually"* (a bank manager).

"I have had two or three extra marital affairs... I have had the best of both the worlds. My wife was hurt by this... but she stood by me... she is a woman of substance" (a government official).

The Strategy of Compromise and Accommodation:

"Compromise, compromise. Compromise is the only secret to a good marriage."

Compromise is used as an effective strategy to deal with all kinds of marital conflicts, tension and dissatisfaction. Professional women more than their husbands compromise on many issues, as they are culturally expected to do so.

As noted earlier, the majority of professional women in this study reported marital satisfaction. Women's professional involvement and psychic satisfaction gained from it have added to their marital satisfaction. This is in consistent with an earlier study conducted by Nathawat and Mathur (1993). The results of their study suggest that for highly educated women, their career facilitates overall marital happiness. Furthermore, university educated professionals view of marriage and its roles are consistent with the Functionalists view of marriage, but they have made some compromises with it, by redesigning it to suit their convenience. Men and women play the instrumental role, as both of them are co-providers, but yet, in domestic sphere, husbands have more authority, decision-making power and importance than wives. Moreover, as Ramu (1987) states, wives' employment has not threatened the traditional superior status of men. In order to preserve marital harmony, professional women do not seem to challenge vehemently the male superiority, but do a skillful balancing act on the tight rope of being both professionals and traditional wives. A way to deal with marital strain is by making *"a man feel like a man."* Again, the attitude of **reconciliation without renunciation** of traditional expectations and "this as well as that" thinking stand out as a strategy for marital harmony. Without drastically changing or challenging their sociocultural circumstances, women have been able to circumnavigate or modify the society's expectations of them. As pointed out by Seymour (1999:275), women are more than passive agents of their sociocultural influences, rather they are able to "shape and transform" their sociocultural system "within the constraints of the prevailing social order and belief system in which they find themselves."

An egalitarian domestic relationship is not the norm among many professional couples; men assume some domestic and more of non-domestic related responsibilities. Their thinking regarding women's traditional role has not radically changed; to some extent they seem to take advantage of the traditional values of their wives. Whereas professional women have made tactical adjustments to their dual roles, without compromising substantially on their traditional roles but making moderate compromise on their professional expectations. They are the ones who are mainly responsible for caring of the children and husbands, extended family members, maintaining a home, cooking, and managing the servants. In addition, they are deferential to their husbands, their parents, and parents-in-law. What has eased the conflict and stress of combining profession and family is the help rendered by the extended family and the servant class.

Jadwin (1992) noticed an interesting feature in her study; one category of women conceal their rejection of social rules, while deliberately imitating female traditional role and virtue in order to avoid social scorn and sanctions.

According to Liddle and Joshi, professional women try not to challenge their male colleagues and also give the "illusion" to their husbands and extended family members that they are submissive (1986:191), to maintain harmonious relationship with their husbands. Women may use some of these cultural expectations as strategies; "submission and silence may be conscious strategies of self-representation deployed when it is expedient to do so, before particular audiences and in particular contexts", argue Raheja and Gold ((1994:11). By creating this "traditional" impression in their husbands and by cleverly balancing both the profession and traditional roles, women in this study have been able to attain their marital satisfaction.

Moreover, professional women's ideology of love, and their expectations of mother and wife role, may have also eased the marital strain, especially for husbands. Remember women's definition of love; love means *"devotion", "dharma," "self-sacrificing," "unselfish," "unconditional," "love is adjustment to whatever problems."* Even as professional women, they are expected to play the *"pathivratha"* role--self-sacrificing and devoted wife and mother roles. They are reminded by their mothers and mothers-in-law, *"not to neglect the family at the cost of pursuing professional ambition."* Menon and Shweder (1998) suggest that Indian women in general attribute their well-being to maintaining social harmony, perpetuation of the extended household and lineage, and fulfilling obligations and duties of their families. Professional women's marital satisfaction seems to be derived from or connected with external factors.

Women may have their own professional identity in the work world, but the cultural scripts suggest that a wife's identity is supposed to merge with her husband's. But in reality, women find satisfaction in retaining their individual identity in the group context. This cultural conditioning may have eased their marital stress, but it can add to their personal stress of combining profession and family, in spite of assistance from the extended family and the servants.

Hindu Rituals:

What has also added to the marital stability and satisfaction of Indian marriages are the innumerable Hindu rituals, festivals, and family cultural traditions. There is a *"pooja"* (sacred prayer) for almost every occasion, celebration, event, and stage in life. There are *"poojas"* to plead and cajole gods and goddesses to favor individuals with blessings and protect them from life's misfortunes. Some may consider these as a nuisance, time consuming and costly affairs. But most subjects feel that Hindu religious rituals strengthen the marital and family bonds, maintain order and stability in the family, act as a cohesive force, and social control. The rituals also remind couples of the prescriptions and proscriptions established by moral-legal Hindu texts (*dharmasastras*) to achieve social harmony and honor within a marriage. Further, they promote integration of nuclear family members with extended family members and reinforcement of marital commitments. They also satisfy psychological needs of couples, especially of women. Hence, couples make less emotional demands on each other. It is noted earlier that Hinduism considers marriage as a holy union for the performance of religious duties. One aim of Hindu marriage is *"dharma"*; here, it refers to the practice of religion and fulfillment of religious obligations.

Relationship baggage:

As indicated earlier, the majority of the respondents (by their own account) with an exception of a small number, were virgins and had an uncomplicated and untarnished past when they came into the marital union. They started their marital lives with deep trust in each other, on a clean slate, without much baggage from previous relationships. The deep trust and stability of relationships bolster their marriage and protect them from mutual suspicion and insecurity. As a female sociologist put it, *"there is no insecurity in arranged marriage... if it is a love marriage, you have fear of rejection in case your husband meets another attractive lady... that fear won't be there in an arranged marriage because of the support from the family."*

Demerits of arranged marriages:

The majority of the respondents have **no** regrets about their arranged marriage. They say *"the strengths are more than weakness,"* but they pointed out **some** of the demerits of arranged marriage.

Inadequate physical and emotional privacy, and Authority structure:

Extended/Joint family-- you can't live with them, you can't live without them!! As the discussion under **Barriers to sexual satisfaction** has already dealt with how the Indian family system affects sexual and marital satisfaction of couples, the discussion here is limited to a few other related issues. The majority of the respondents acknowledge the beneficial role of the extended family members in the stability of their marriages and appreciate their help in childcare and socialization, as pointed out earlier. They appreciate the strong social support given by them to alleviate marital strain. Nevertheless, many also think that inadequate privacy, both physical and emotional, and the invasive nature of the extended family members, are some of the major disadvantages of Indian marriages which add to the marital stress and even affects general well-being. These issues are related to the authority structure of the family. It may be reminded here, that it is not uncommon for married couples and extended family members to co-reside for economic considerations and to fulfill parental obligations.

Respondents think marital satisfaction could be vastly improved if the married people could live separately, and have more emotional privacy and less intrusive extended family members. But complete alienation of or isolation from one's extended family is not seen as an option in order to improve marital happiness. Those who co-reside with their extended family members, but have an autonomous life and have a compatible relationship with the extended family, have **no** complaints about them.

Excessive control of married couples by the apparently intrusive elder family members is seen as a problem by some. Marital choice, marital freedom, marital decisions and interactions are thwarted to a certain extent by the good intentioned elders. It is sociologically well known that in rural joint families, husband and wife interaction is restricted to promote the cohesiveness of the larger family. But among urban educated families, there is more sensitivity and respect for marital autonomy and privacy than rural joint families. Nevertheless, the problem of elders interference and control seriously affects those couples who have restricted physical and emotional space as result of co-residing with their extended family members. But, it also affects those couples who do not co-reside with their extended family, but have close associations and connections with the extended family members. For women, the stress of combining profession and family is exacerbated; as women they are expected to conform to the expectations of both their conjugal family and extended family. In addition to the responsibility of maintaining well-being and harmony in their families and acting as integrating force, they are also expected to perform their professional duties.

In this study, more women expressed some dissatisfaction with their extended family structure than men respondents in open comments during the interviews. Although Chand's (1989) study did not deal only with university educated women, she found a higher number of women associated their poor marital satisfaction with mother-in-law problems than men. Women seem to favor conjugal love/nuclear family structure as it provides them marital autonomy and privacy, while creating a safe zone from conflict with joint/extended family and less responsibilities towards them. Several ethnographic evidence, psychoanalysis of women, and analysis of oral traditions support the view that women desire conjugal relationships over joint family, exclusive relationships with their husbands, and autonomous marital life that excludes the extended family (Kakar (1989), Raheja and Gold (1994), Derné (1995), Ingham (1996), Puri (1999). Raheja and Gold's analysis of oral traditions in the form of songs, indicate "the desirability of disrupting patrilineal unity in favor of a stress on conjugality" (Ibid.,:20). Similarly, Ingham's analysis of oral traditions (Ibid.:579) point out women's desire for "satisfying relationship" with their husbands. Puri's (Ibid:) analysis of her female subjects' narratives suggest that women seem to favor companionate marriage–marriage that has elements of intimacy, love, mutual emotional attachment.

Lamb offers a plausible explanation about the desire in women for conjugal relationship and independence. Indian family structure and customs require the newly married women transfer their loyalty from their parents' household to their husbands' household, unlike newly married men. "Because she must shift her allegiance from one group to another, a woman may be more likely to develop a sense of independence from any particular group. Women may focus on independence and self-reliance precisely because they do not have the same sense of group protection that men do" (1997; 289-91). Kakar (1981) attributes this desire to the girls' socialization which is different from the boys. While these studies may not be directly linked to the university-educated urban professional women, they offer a general view of women.

The elders invasive nature into the marital affairs of their children is related to the authority structure. As alluded to earlier, even among the educated class, family relationships are based on hierarchy with the older people with males occupying higher position of importance and power than younger women. By virtue of the fact that elders occupy higher position in the family authority structure, they feel they must exercise their authority. In this study, **some** professional women who co-reside with their extended family members feel that in spite of their university education and economic independence, they feel that they are still at the bottom of the family authority structure. The culture demands that they conform to their traditional female role of being compliant, respectful, passive, and obedient to their husbands and older males and females. They may have their self-identity in the professional world, but in their domestic role, as traditions expect, their identity is expected to merge with their husbands, is consistent with the Hindu concept of *"ardhangi"* (the other half). But, there is less talk or less concern among professional women about the loss of self-identity, autonomy and free will; these Western issues are not given as much importance as they are given in Western societies. Despite limited focus on these issues, professional women have done a remarkable job of integrating family and profession, and also have risen to positions of power and importance. Perhaps not overanalyzing the issues of self-identity and autonomy is a coping strategy to reduce marital strain or they might have found their identity actualized in the group context. As Kakar (1981:56) notes that an Indian woman's "identity is wholly defined by relationship to others as a daughter, as a wife and as a mother."

Professional men and women are caught between filial piety and obligations to the elderly, and preserving their own marital autonomy and marital satisfaction. On the other hand, the extended family members are also caught between exercising their filial authority in order to promote the marital stability, and granting autonomy to their married children... *"We know what is best for you"* is their slogan, based on their wisdom and life experience. *"Some couples are not happy because of lack of individual development"; "there is lack of freedom and individuality"* due to the control of the elders, commented respondents.

This supports other research findings on collectivist societies. Suh and Oishi (2002), in their analysis of Subjective Well-Being Across Cultures find individualist cultures are happier than collectivists. One of the important elements that play a key role in their experiencing higher subjective well-being than collectivists is their personal freedom and freedom of choice about different aspects of their lives. Furthermore, in collectivist societies individuals have to sublimate their interests, wishes, thoughts, and choices to their significant in-group, like extended family. There is less freedom to follow one's own dream or rewarding personal goals. Moreover, as Triandis (2000) notes, collectivism is correlated with tightness resulting in lower subjective well-being. He states tight cultures have many rules and norms, and deviation from them meets strict sanction from the group members. Professional women and men of this study have conflicts with their extended family members and also experience certain anxiety and pressure due to the societal pressure on them to show deferential, obedient, and caring behavior towards their elder family members. Non-conformists may be dealt with social sanction and criticism. In order to preserve the cohesiveness of the family, the elders exercise double standard of social control; they are more critical of their female family members than male members. There is a higher social conformity bar for females than males.

In this study, there is no documentation on correlation between low self-esteem among the subjects and their lower subjective well-being, as a result of living in collectivistic society. But one can speculate based on the research findings of other collectivist societies. Suh and Oishi (2002) research suggest that self-esteem, self-consistency appear to be correlated to happiness in individualist/Western cultures rather than in collectivist cultures. In collectivist cultures such as India, even professional women in domestic sphere are expected to maintain self-sacrificing, deferential, congenial, harmonious relationships with their husbands, children, and the elder family members. While in their professional world, they are expected to be rational, goal-oriented, competent, and efficient. Suh and Oishi argue that this kind of traditional behavior with the family requires the self to be highly sensitive to others and adjust the self to the needs and expectations of others. This self-flexibility that demands the self to adjust to both traditional and professional roles may be a hindrance to consistent self-identity, hence to lower well-being. Furthermore, the society is more critical of women than men who are nonconformists to traditional values. The ability to maintain a consistent self-identity is seen as an important factor in the subjective well-being of individuals in individualist societies in Suh and Oishi's research. Similarly, Kakar (1992) speculates, Indian gainfully employed married women and mothers are likely to experience severe inner psychological struggle as a result of deviating from the norm of being a devoted ideal wife/mother.

Some women think, "*some women suffer in arranged marriages*". How? Because of the power dynamics. "*Husbands become authoritarian, because their family/mothers influence him in his marital decisions*" (a female professor of Economics). "*Sometimes in-laws influence their sons, and they develop negative feelings towards their wives.*" A female physician is surprised that her professional husband defends his mother unobjectively.

> "*Husbands could become authoritarian in an arranged marriage, in the extended family setup. In love marriages, there is equality between husbands and wives... you have your own individuality. Arranged marriage is a lucky dip...(lottery)...husbands' ideas, attitudes become more important than yours*" (a female program executive).

It should be noted here that in **Chap. 4.** under **Barriers to Sexual Enjoyment and Satisfaction in Arranged Marriage,** there is discussion on the complex relationships of mothers and sons and mothers-in-law and daughters-in-law. In this section, further discussion on the same issue continues. Mothers-in-law are not seen as agents of control and domination follows by most professional women; nevertheless, **some** women stated there are conflicts between them and their mothers-in-law. Mothers-in-law appreciate their daughters-in-law professional involvement and the second income they bring to the family, but at the same time there is a conflict between them and their daughters-in-law. As the latter try to assert the values of individualism, independence, and marital autonomy associated with their education and economic independence, it leads to conflict. Professional women who are highly motivated to advance professionally are reminded by their mothers and mothers-in-law about their traditional expectations – to be a good wife and a good mother. *"Don't pursue professional advancement at the cost of neglecting your husband and children's welfare."* They are "expected" to act like a *pativratha* (virtuous wife), emulating the lives of legendary *pathivratas* of ancient literature, such as *Savitri, Sita.* Even if the professional women have liberated themselves from such cultural expectations and constraints, they have internalized these values that may cause stress of combining profession and family. As mothers/wives, they are expected to integrate the family and maintain harmony.

Conflict with mothers-in-law cause marital problems, marital dissatisfaction, and professional distraction for those with whom mothers-in-law co-reside. *"Sometimes mothers-in-law are dominant, they boss over their daughters-in-law... they are awful... they think they have authority over us,"* says another woman. *"Even if it is a simple action, like bringing a female friend home, you have to think about your in-laws who live with us... no independence to do what you want to do."* (a female professor). This corroborates Puri's finding, that women experience loss of freedom and have social constraints in conjugal families. Conjugal family refers to "the family unit within which women marry and live, which may include members of the husband's family (1999:150,137). Mothers-in-law try to exercise power over their daughters-in-law, as they occupy higher position in the family hierarchy than daughters-in-law. Brown (1982,1992) and Sacks (1992), conclude from analyzing many cross cultural studies that as women grow older, they begin to have male privileges and prerogatives such as power, status, and autonomy. Lamb (2000:66) notes that as senior family members age, they may move to the powerless peripheries of their households, but they "maintain their hierarchical position as superiors." It can also be argued that powerless peripheral position of older family members makes them assert their lost status, hence they control the younger people through their rebuke, criticism, and complaint.

Even if mothers do not co-reside with their married sons, they could control their sons through "remote control," if the sons are emotionally dependent on their mothers. This dependency is likely to cause marital strain and absence of emotional intimacy between husbands and wives. Women commented:

"My husband is the last son and very much attached to his mother... he spends a lot of time with her... since I had the baby. She controls him... he will do whatever she wants him to do..."

"mother-in-law becomes jealous of her daughter-in-law and feels she is losing her son."

"he always listens to his mother more than me."

As noted earlier, Indian scholars have observed and written about the excessive attachment of Indian males with their mothers and emotional dependency on them. De, a popular novelist characterizes the urban Indian male as "ill-mannered, overgrown child, spoilt rather socialized by his mother" (Dwyer : 2000:205). Sons are sandwiched between their wives and mothers, who demand equal affection and attention, equal time, equal privileges, equal economic considerations. But, more than anything else, wives and mothers-in-law compete with each for their son's and husband's affection and loyalty; each tries to influence their sons/husbands in family's crucial decisions.

The domestic power dynamics and intrigue affect men also. A man voiced the opinions of other men who are caught between the cross fire of their mothers, mothers-in-law, wives, sisters, sisters-in-law:

"Women fight with each other for petty things... they become jealous of each other and compete with each other... fighting over trivial things... they strain the marital relationship."

So, how do you deal with all these internal conflicts and power struggles? As one woman, put it, *"you have to compromise many things in an arranged marriage."*

It is also noted by respondents of this study that the individuals do not take personal responsibility in an arranged marriage; *"in love marriages, when they can't live together, they go for a divorce, but in arranged marriage, when things go wrong, they blame the elders who arranged the marriage." "You are not responsible for everything that goes wrong in an arranged marriage."* Despite the fact most respondents think that the extended family is a fortifying force of marital stability, some think, *"by interfering into marital lives of their children, they superficially straighten the marriages"* (a female program executive). A female physician says, *"for appearance sake and to protect the family's name, sometimes couples with marital problems have to maintain pseudo relationship." "They can't walk out of marriage, because they have to think about their parents... they think it is shameful to get a divorce"* (a male professor).

Although the extended family is beneficial to the success of marriages, nevertheless, individuals are aware of the problems created by its invasiveness nature that result in compromising their individual interests and goals. Several scholars such as Shukla (1987) Mines (1988) have recognized that individual ideologies, desires, beliefs, and practices tend to be circumscribed by the cultural ideals and social expectations of family stability, harmony, cooperation, conformity and filial piety. Nevertheless, men and women of this study have an attitude of **reconciliation without renunciation** even dealing with their extended/ joint family.

Limited Egalitarian Relationship:

As noted earlier, women continue to play traditional roles in spite of their professional involvement. Interestingly, most women didn't complain about the limited egalitarian relationship between them and their husbands in domestic sphere. Such is the powerful internalization of cultural values and norms that promote and preserve male's privileged status and gender segregated roles. An ideal wife/mother is expected to be self-sacrificing, patient and play multiple roles with competency and efficiency combined with tolerance for their husband's reluctance to share housework. At times, some of them act like "bell-hops" to meet the demands of their family members. This immensely pleases the husbands while increasing role conflict, time pressure, and stress for women.

Men did not report that their wives insist that they should have more egalitarian relationship between them in domestic responsibilities. The patriarchal traditions and male/female role compartmentalization of activities continue to prevail even among the university educated class in spite of modernization and urbanization. Professional women are the primary caregivers and assume more domestic responsibilities than their husbands. Ramu, in his study of dual-career families, notes that Indian husbands have been most resistant to change in the area of participation in domestic duties. He contends in Indian society, the cultural and religious beliefs that males and females have "natural" propensities for competency in gender segregated work continue to prevail. Men have shown modern attitude in approving of their wives' employment, which is an economic asset to the family. But they protect their traditional role and have developed "cultivated incompetence" in domestic role (1987). There is also "cultivated blindness" that some men use to their advantage–they can't find anything in their home unless their wives find it for them.

Economic Interdependency:

The extended family may have an ulterior motive in protecting the stability of marriages of their children. Concerns about stigma, loss of social prestige, and financial resources in case of marriage breakup, are not unreal. The elders who arrange the marriage are *"self-interested people,"* some said. They see marriage as a strategy to improve their own economic status and augment their economic resources; an eligible bachelor with professional education and high income is considered as an asset to the entire family. So are the career women; *"people want to improve their standard of living through career women"* says a professional woman. A female physician talked about how the in-laws and her husband put pressure on her to complete a specialization, rather than have a baby ! so that she could bring in a higher income. Other women mentioned how parents make a deliberate attempt to seek career women for their sons. Quite often money is the main source of conflict between the couples, and the couples and their extended family members.

It is not only the parents who have some economic motivation in arranged marriages, but also the marriage suitors. *"It is the economic necessity that made me go through arranged marriage"* says a radio station executive. Marrying into money is seen as a strategy to increase one's own economic resources and improve social standing. There is economic interdependency between the extended family and married couples; economic resources are pooled together in order to maximize their benefit. As indicated earlier in the section on **Socialization,** family relations with "long-term bonds of reciprocal indebtedness and interdependence" (Lamb, 2000:46,47) is an important feature of the Indian society. This cultural aspect is mutually beneficial to both the younger and the older generations, but it can also lead to interpersonal conflicts; *"because of financial interdependency... people don't get out of marriage... they suffer,"* stated subjects of this study who had conflicts with their parents.

A suitable son-in-law or daughter-in-law from *"Bhadralok"* or *"people of good family,"* not only adds to the reputation and social prestige of the extended family, but also enhances or increases their economic asset. An obsession with "good family" and socio/economic similarities results sometimes in ignoring the interests and wishes of young people. There are cases even among educated middle and upper classes where young people agree to marry because of parental pressure. They go through a wedding extravaganza and then decide to annul marriage or abandon the marital partner or divorce. When they are asked about the reason for marriage dissolution, they state the parents pressured them to marry someone against their wishes. But the same people did not have the courage to stand up to their parents before the marriage; *"I couldn't deal with the family pressure"; "I didn't want to disappoint my parents, because the wedding arrangements were already made"; "I was afraid of bringing shame and dishonor to my family"* are some of the reasons. An Indian professional with a Ph.D. living in the U.S.A. married a woman of his *"mother's choice"* in India, after he was engaged to her for six months. Then he dissolved the marriage just a couple of months after his wife joined him in the U.S.A., because he *"didn't find her sexually attractive"; "my mother said, she was 5ft.2," actually she was 4ft.11"* (he measured her height with a measuring tape !).

This study does not have documentation on the number of people who received and gave dowry. Although *dowry,* per se, is not the norm among professionals, a handsome "gift" to the bridegroom in the form of materialistic goods (car, house, household appliances) is a form of *de facto dowry.* Some respondents of this study revealed their concern about this social evil and how it affects marital satisfaction:

"Women are harassed by men if they don't bring in a dowry". "Aversion, hatred develop between husbands and wives when the expected dowry is not delivered."

"If women are harassed for dowry, they will not develop sexual attraction towards their husbands."

"Women feel husbands are money minded... she doesn't like sex with him, because she is treated like a commodity."

"She won't be relaxed sexually if she is under pressure from the in-laws about dowry."

"There is chronic antagonism between mother-in-law and daughter-in-law, because of unmet expectations of dowry."

An expensive wedding, dowry or bride and bride groom gifts also saddle parents with heavy debt, increasing their financial stress and relationship problems with others.

Sexual Satisfaction and Personality Conflict:

As indicated earlier, the majority of respondents reported that they developed sexual attraction slowly and gradually, and they also report sexual satisfaction in their marriages, but a small number of them (5%) have no sexual attraction or satisfaction. They feel the cause for this is arranged marriage; *"One has to love a person in order to experience sexual pleasure... in arranged marriage, you are not passionately involved with your husband,"* says a woman who was romantically involved with another man, before she married her present husband through arranged marriage. Individuals recognize the importance of sexual attraction for marital satisfaction:

"In an arranged marriage, if you are not sexually attracted it could be a major barrier for marital satisfaction. If the elders impose marriage against your will, it could be disastrous. Sexual attraction between husband and wife is very important."

"Sexual attraction has a positive effect on marriage. Otherwise, it will be difficult... you'll be drifting sexually."

A few of them would prefer romantic marriages if they were to do it all over again. Why ?

> *"because of premarital sex and you can get to know the personality of the other";*
>
> *"for sexual enjoyment, love marriage is good because it is based on sexual attraction";*
>
> *"Arranged marriage is a gamble, there is no chance to get to know the personality of each other... in love marriage, there is more acquaintance and understanding of each other."*
>
> *"I recommend love marriage because there is a better mutual*

understanding."

"Falling in love is more exciting than arranged marriage."

Those who were not engaged or had a chance to become acquainted with each other before the marriage promoted the idea of a long engagement:

"The families should give young people time to get to know each other... understand each other before the marriage and they should give a chance for them to break up if they want to";

"You know a person briefly and you take on that person as your marital partner for life ? This is a weakness in arranged marriages."

"They (parents) don't understand, we should get a chance to know each other before getting married."

A period of engagement is recommended as it also promotes sexual compatibility and satisfaction; *"time should be given before marriage to develop romantic feelings."* Also, they think an extended period of engagement would give them a chance to fall in love; *"if I had fallen in love with my husband before marriage, it would have been better."* It may be reminded here, the **Before Marriage Group,** who were sexually attracted to each other before their marriage and also had a period of engagement, reported higher sexual satisfaction then the **After Marriage Group.**

Potential marital partners may have all the similarities, but that does not assure them mutual familiarity and understanding of each other at the beginning of the marriage. This is a common problem, that most couples have to deal with. But with time, they are able to make an emotional connection because of shared marital life and shared similarities. There are also personality and temperament clashes, as a female professor of sociology put it, *"because of different socialization."* While the marriage is being arranged, there is a de-emphasis on psychological profile of potential marital partners and their psychological compatibility, which results in marital strain later. Different socialization and different family values, life styles, ideas, and attitudes lead to conflict between the extended family members and sons-in-law and daughters-in-law. *"Sometimes it is so difficult to adjust to the family you are married into."* An arranged marriage does not fully guarantee similarity of attitudes and life styles between the in-laws.

Loss of Freedom of Choice:

Although **no** respondent reported coerced arranged marriage and they married marital partners whom they like, but yet, there is a strong belief in *"we should have a choice,"* even among individuals who have a good marriage. A man who rates his marriage as 7 on a scale of 1-10, says, *"if I were to do it all over again, I want to have my own choice... I want to fall in love."* A male English professor summed up, *"arranged marriage is good, as long as there is a choice for you... and your marital partner is not thrust upon you."* Some resent *"total dependency on others in the most important decision of your life."* Another man, who was heavily influenced by his mother in his marital choice, talked about the lack of excitement in arranged marriage:

> *"I had no freedom of choice, because my mother's words became very important. I would have liked to choose my own. In arranged marriage, there is not much excitement, because you know for a long time whom you are going to marry."*

Some women and men felt that *"a woman's opinion regarding her marital partner is given less importance than a man's."* In arranged marriage parlance, grown-up men and women with university education and economic self-sufficiency are referred to as "boys" and "girls." The choice of words, *"they are looking for a girl/boy"* suggest that potential marriage suitors are not mature enough to make independent decisions about their marriage, hence they have to be guided like children.

A serious criticism comes from a woman, who is terribly unhappy with her marriage and her *"disastrous sex life"*:

"I resented the fact that I had to get married through arranged marriage. I suppressed my feelings... marriage was imposed on me. I didn't have a negative attitude towards sex, but towards the man whom I married."

Hocuspocus Horoscope:

Even among the educated class, the force of traditions insist that the two potential marital partners' horoscope should match for a good marriage and therefore, astrologers should be consulted **before** wedding plans are finalized. Some view this as a part of the marriage ritual, but many orthodox Hindus take it rather seriously. A couple may have all the similarities and a have mutual desire to get married, but as stated earlier, if the astrologers think the horoscope of the intended couple is not compatible, the deal is off. The superstitious, money-motivated astrologers construct and interpret and reinterpret horoscopes. Their interpretation is "adjustable" and can completely derail the wedding plans and violate the wishes of the potential marital partners. By manipulating the interpretation of the horoscope, the astrologers can make or break a marriage plan and realign the potential candidates with others to suit the other competing party's wishes or to enrich their own pockets.

"Too much stress on astrology...horoscope, hence they discourage the wish of the couple who may happen to like each other... their opinion is not taken seriously".

In-breeding:

Marriage between niece and uncle, between maternal cousins or second cousins, between sisters from one family and brothers from another family is culturally accepted. Even though this inter-family marriage is not common, but yet it is practiced in order to keep the economic resources within the family and to maintain the cohesiveness of the extended family. Besides, marrying "one of us" ensures stability of the marriage.

But, this extended family endogamous marriage is criticized by some respondents as *"an incestuous relationship,"* resulting in sexual dysfunctions. *"My sister married my uncle. She can't bring herself to make love to him, because he is her uncle!"* A male biologist thinks a serious weakness of arranged marriage is *"inner breeding that results in mental retardation, deformation etc...."* Another male biologist who is equally critical of this custom said: *"in a sense, arranged marriages are incestuous, I belong to a small community... they all look alike !"*

A male journalist's views seem to represent the majority opinion on the merits and demerits of arranged marriage:

"Arranged marriage is very good, ***but*** *if there is no choice... if somebody insists that you should marry* ***this*** *particular person, then it is not correct. If the option or choice is given to* ***both*** *man and woman...then if they agree...along with parents consent, then arranged marriage is a better way..."*

At the end of this discussion of **Sexuality and love in arranged marriages: Why arranged marriages last,** a few major conclusions may be made:

Despite the fact the subjects of this study are university-educated professionals, Indian cultural values and the extended family have a powerful influence on them in their decision to op for arranged marriage. Cultural scripts continue to shape and determine, dictate their choice of marital partner, their "first night", and other aspects of marital life. The institution of arranged marriage continues to exist with tenacity and rigidity, in spite of modernization and urbanization. As long as the caste system exists, so will the arranged marriage system.

While love and sexual attraction before marriage may be necessary for an enjoyable "first night" and marital sexual satisfaction, they may not be absolutely essential in the decision to choose a marital partner. Why? Sexual attraction and love could be constructed, cultivated and concocted, as long as there are socio-cultural similarities and other compatibilities. Nevertheless, the presence of love and sexual attraction before the marriage are contributory factors in higher sexual satisfaction. The **Before-Marriage Group** reported higher sexual satisfaction than the **After-Marriage Group.** But, yet the majority of the total respondents report that they have a good marriage and marital satisfaction and have no regrets about their arranged marriage, in spite of not having feelings of love or sexual attraction at the beginning of their meeting each other.

What makes a good marriage? Why do arranged marriages last? The extended family's support system; the low, but realistic expectations of marriage and marital partners; the definition of love; the dominant force of cultural values; unfailing and unyielding commitment; and professional women's skillful strategy in combining traditional role with their traditional role are some of the important factors in the high survivability of arranged marriages.

"There is really not much difference between arranged marriages and love/romantic marriages, as long as there are elements of a good marriage..."

BIBLIOGRAPHY

Ahuja, Ram (1993). *Indian Social System.* New Delhi:Rawat Publications.

Aron, A. and E. Aron. (1991). Love and Sexuality. In *Sexuality in Close Relationships,* ed. K. McKinney and S. Sprecher. Hillsdale, N.J. : Lawrence Erlbaum Associates.

Aron, A., and Westbay, L. (1996) Dimensions of the prototype of love. *Journal of Personality and Social Psychology.* 70:535-51.

Aron, A., M/Paris, and E.N. Aron. (1995). Falling in Love: Prospective studies of self-concept change. *Journal of Personality and Social Psychology.* I 69:1102-12.

Aronson, E. (1998). The *Social animal.* (7th ed.). San Francisco : Freeman.

Bailey, F.G. (1991). Religion and Religiosity : Ideas and Their Use. In *Contributions in Indian Sociology.* 25:211-232.

Basu, Monmayee. (2001). *Hindu women and Marriage Law: From Sacrament to Contract.* New Delhi: Oxford University Press.

Bellah, R.N., Madsen R., Sullivan. W.M., Swidler, A.,Tipton, S.M. (1991) *The Good Society.* New York:Knoff.

Bhattacharya, G. (2000), *Sexuality and Society.* New York: Routledge.

Brown, Judith. (1982), Cross-Cultural perspectives on middle-aged women. *Current Anthropology.* 23:143-56.

Brown, Judith. (1992). Lives of middle-aged women. In *In her prime: New views of middle aged women.* Ed. by Virginia Kerns and Judith Brown. 17-32. Urbana: University of Illinois Press.

Burgess, E.W., and Locke, H.J. (1963). *The Family.* New York: American Book.

Buss, D.M. (1985), "Human mate selection", *American Scientist,* 73,47-51.

Buss, D.M., Abbott, M., Angleitner, A., & Asherian, A. (1990). International preferences in mate selection : Evolutionary hypothesis tested in 37 cultures. *Behavioral and Brain Sciences,* 12,1-49.

Collins, Randall. (1988). The Durkheimian Tradition in Conflict Sociology. p.p. 107-128. *Durkheimian Sociology: Cultural Studies.* J.C.Alexander ed. Cambridge: Cambridge University Press.

Chand, Meena Suraiya. (1989). *An Inquiry into the factors of a successful marriage.* Ph.D. dissertation. Jadavpur University. India.

Cowgill,Donald.(1979). Aging and Modernization: A Revision of the Theory. In *Late Life : Communities and Environmental Policy.* Ed. J.Gubrium. Springfield,Ill.: Charles C. Thomas, Publisher.

Danielou,Alain. (1994). The Complete Kama Sutra Translation. Rochester, Vermont : Park Street Press.

Davis, Kingsley. (1941). Intermarriage in Caste Societies. *American Anthropologist.* 43:385-395.

Davenport,W.H. (1977). Sex in cross-cultural perspective. In F.A. Beach (ed.), *Human Sexuality in four perspectives.* pp115-164. Baltimore: John Hopkins Univeristy Press.

Das,Veena. (1993) Masks and Faces. In *Family, Kinship, Marriage in India.* Ed.P.Uberoi. New Delhi: Oxford University Press.

DeLamater, John. (1987) Gender differences in sexual scenarios. In K. Kelley (Ed.), *Females, males, and sexuality: Theories of Research.127-140.* Albany, N.y. : SUNY Press.

DeLamater, John (1991) Emotions and Sexuality. In *Sexuality in Close Relationships.* McKinney, K.& Sprecher, S. (Eds.) Hillside, N.J.: Lawrence Erlbaum Associate Publications.

De Munck, Victor (1998) Lust, Love, and Arranged Marriages in Sri Lanka. In *Romantic Love and Sexual Behavior.* New York:Praeger

Derné,Steve. (1994). Hindu men talk about controlling women : cultural ideas as a tool of the powerful. *Sociological Perspectives.* Summer, v. 37, n 2,.p 203. (25).

________ (1994). Arranging Marriage: How Father's Concerns Limit Women's Educational Achievements. In *Women, Education and Family Structure in India.* Mukhopadhyay and Seymour (eds.). Oxford: Westview Press.

________ (1995). *Culture in Action- Family Life, Emotion and Male Dominance in Banaras, India.* State University of New York Press.

Diener, E. (2000). Subjective well-being: The science of happiness, and a proposal for national index. *American Psychologist,* 55, 34-43.

Dion, K., & Dion, K. (1993). Individualistic and collectivistic perspectives on gender and the cultural context of love and intimacy. *Journal of Social*

Issues, Fall 1993,49.

Dumont, Louis. (1970). *Homo Hierarchicus:The Caste System and Its Implications.* Chicago: University of Chicago Press.

Dwyer,Rachel. (2000). *All You Want Is Money, All You need is Love.* London and New York: Cassell.

Fisher, Helen. (2004) *Why We Love. The Nature and Chemistry of Romantic Love.* New York: Henry Holt and company.

Fisher, Helen. (1992) *Anatomy of Love.* New York:W.W.Norton and Co.

Foucault, M. (1978) *A History of Sexuality:* vol.1. *An Introduction.* New York:Pantheon.

Freud, Sigmund. (1905). *Three Essays on the Theory of Sexuality* In Freud 1953-74, vol.7.

Gagnon, J.H.,& W. Simon. (1973) *Sexual Conduct : The Social Sources of Human Sexuality.* New York: Aldine de Gruyter.

Gore, M.S., (1968) *Urbanization and Family Change.* Bombay : Popular Prakashan

Goode, W.J. (1959) The theoretical importance of love. *American Sociological Review,* 24,38-47.

Gough, Kathleen (1993) Brahman Kinship in a Tamil Village. In *Family, Kinship, Marriage in India.* Ed.P.Uberoi. New Delhi:Oxford university Press.

Gupta, Giri (1976). Love, Arranged Marriage, and the Indian Social Structure. *Journal of Comparative Family Studies.* vol.7,1, Spring, 75-85.

Gupta, V. and Singh, P. (1982) in D.G. Meyers, *Social Psychology,* 4th ed.,1993,p.495. New York:McGraw-Hill.

Harlan, Lindsey. (1992). *Religion and Rajput Women: The Ethic of Protection in Contemporary Narratives.* Berkeley: University of California Press.

Harlan, Lindsey & Courtright, Paul (1995). *From the Margins of Hindu Marriage: Essays on Gender, Religion, and Culture.* New York, Oxford: Oxford University Press.

Hartfield, E. & Rapson, R.L. (1993). *Love Sex and Intimacy: Their Biology, Psychology and History.* New York : Harper Collins.

Hatfield, E. (1988) Passionate Love and Companionate Love. In Sternberg, R. & Barners, M. (eds.) *The Psychology of Love.* 191-217. New Haven; Yale

University Press.

Homans, George C. (1961). *Social Behavior:Its Elementary Forms.* New York : Harcourt, Brace and World.

Ingham, J. (1996). 'Oedipality in pragmatic dicourse: Trobriands and Hindu India'. In *Ehos*, 24,559-87.

Jadwin, Lisa (1992) The Seductiveness of Female Duplicity in *Vanity Fair. Studies in English Literature.* 32:663-687.

Kane, P.V. (1941a.) *History of Dharmasastra,* vol. 2, part 1. Poona; Bhandarkar Oriental Research Institute.

Kapadia, K.M. (1966). *Marriage and Family in India,* 3rd ed. Bombay:Oxford University Press.

Kapur, Promila. (1972). *Marriage and the working women in India.* New Delhi: Vikas Publishing Co.

Kakar, Sudhir. (1992) *The Inner World,* New Delhi: Oxford University Press.

________ (1989, 1990) *Intimate Relations : Exploring Indian Sexuality.* New Delhi: Viking.

_________ (1978/1981) *The Inner World: a Psycho-analytic Study of Childhood and Society in India.* New Delhi : Oxford University Press.

Khare, R.S. (1982). From Kanya to Mata:Aspects of the Cultural Language of Kinship in Northern India. In *Concepts of Person: Kinship, Caste, and Marriage in India.* Ed. by Ostor,A., Fruzzetti, L., Barnett, S.

Kitayama, S. and Markus H.R. (2000). The Pursuit of Happiness and the Realization of Sympathy: Cultural patterns of Self, Social Relations, and Well-being. In *Culture and Subjective Well-being.* Ed. by E. Diener and E.M. Suh. (2000). Cambridge: The MIT Press.

Kolenda, Pauline (1978). *Caste in Contemporary India; Beyond Organic Solidarity.* Menlo Park,California: The Benjamin/Cummings Publishing Co.

Kolenda, Pauline (2003). *Caste, Marriage, and Inequality: Essays on North and South India.* New Delhi: Rawat Publications.

Kon,I.S. (1987) A Sociological approach. In J.H. Geer & W.T. O'Donohue (Eds.), *Theories of human sexuality* (pp.257-286). New York : Plenum Press.

Kumar, P. & Makwana, S. (1991). Factors affecting sexual satisfaction in married life. *Journal of the Indian Academy of Applied Psychology. Vo.17.(1-2)31-34.*

Kulahar, P. & Avasthi, A. (1995) Sexual dysfunction in the Indian subcontinent. *International Review of Psychiatry. vol.7.(2)23-239.*

Kurtz, Stanley (1992). *All the Mothers are One: Hindu India and the Cultural Shaping of Psychoanalysis.* New York: Columbia University Press.

Lamb, Sarah (2000). *White Saris and Sweet Mangoes; Aging, Gender and Body in North India.* Berkeley: University of California Press.

_______ (1997) 'The making and unmaking of persons: Notes on aging and gender in North India'. In *Ethos*, 25,279-302.

Laumann, E.O., R.T. Michael, and J.H. Gagnon (1994). *The Social Organization of Sexuality: Sexual Practices in the United States.* Chicago : University of Chicago Press.

Laumann. E.O., & Gagnon J.H. (1995).A Sociological Perspective on Sexual Action. In *Conceiving Sexuality: Approaches to sex research in a postmodern world.* Ed. Parker.R.,& Gagnon,G.H. New York:Routledge.

Laumann, E.O. (2004). *Sexual Organization of the City.* Chicago: University of Chicago.

Lee,J.A., (1973). *The Colors of Love: An Exploration of the Ways of Loving.* Toronto : New Press.

Lee,J.A. (1977). A typology of styles of loving. *Personality and Social Psychology Bulletin,* 3, 173-182.

Levine, R., Sato, S., Hashimoto, T., Verma, J. (1995), Love and Marriage in Eleven Cultures. *Journal of Cross-Cultural Psychology.* Vol. 26.5, Sept.

Liddle, Joanna., and Joshi,Rama.1986. *Daughters of Independence: Gender, Caste and Class in India.* New Brunswick: Rutgers University Press.

Liebowitz, M.R.(1983). *The Chemistry of Love.* Boston : Little, Brown.

Lumpert, Ada.(1997). *The Evolution of Love.* Westport, CT : Praeger.

Markus, H.R., and Kitayama,S. (1991) Culture and the self : Implications for cognition, emotion, and motivation. *Psychological Review.* 98:224:53.

Markus, H.R., and Kitayama, S. (1994), The cultural construction of the self and emotion:Implications for social behavior. *In S.Kitayama and H.R.*

Markus,eds., Emotion and Culture: Empirical Studies of Mutual Influence. American Psychological Association, pp.89-130.

Mehta, Ram (1973) Is the joint family breaking up? *The Illustrated Weekly of India,* xciv, sept.23:631-646.

Menon, U. and Shweder, R.A. (1998). The return of the "white man's burden": The moral discourse of anthropology and the domestic life of Hindu women. In R.A. Shweder, ed. *Welcome to Middle Age!(and other cultural fictions).* pp. 139-88. Chicago: University of Chicago Press.

Menon, U.,and Shweder, R.,(1994). Kali's Tongue: Cultural Psychology and the Power of "Shame" in Orissa, India. In S.Kitayama and H.Markus (eds.) *Emotion and Culture: Empirical Studies of Mutual Influence.* P.p.241-284. Washington, D.C. APA Books.

Meyer,J.J. (1995). *Sexual Life in Ancient India.* New York: Dorset Press

Michael, R.T., Gagnon J.H., Laumann, E.O. and Kolata, G (1994) *Sex in America: A Definitive survey.* New York: Warner Books.

Mines, Diane and Lamb, Sarah. Eds. (2002). *Everyday Life in South Asia.* Bloomington: Indiana University Press.

Mines, Mattison. (1994). *Public Faces, Private Voices: Community and Individuality in South India.* Berkeley: University of California Press.

_______ (1988). 'Conceptualizing the person: Hierarchical society and individual autonomy in India'. In *American Anthropologist,* 90, 568-79.

Mitter, Sara. (1991). *Dharma's Daughters: Contemporary Indian Women and Hindu Culture.* New Brunswick: Rutgers University Press.

Money, J. (1986) *Lovemaps : Clinical Concepts of Sexual/Erotic Health and Pathology Parphilia and Gender Transposition in Childhood, Adolescence and Maturity.* New York:Irvington.

Mukhopadhyay, Carol. & Seymour, Susan (eds.) (1994). *Women, Education and Family Structure in India.* Oxford: Westview Press.

Murstein, Bernard I. (1980). Mate Selection in the 1970s. *Journal of Marriage and the Family.* 42:777-792.

Nag,Moni. (1996) *Sexual Behavior and Aids in India.* New Delhi:Vikas Publishing House.

Nagpal, Ashok. (2003). 'Cultural Continuity and Change in Kakar's Works: Some Reflections'. In *Childhood, Family, And Sociocultural Change in*

India: Reinterpreting the Inner World. Dinesh Sharma (ed.). New Delhi: Oxford University Press.

Nair, Janaki. & John,Mary. (1998). *A Question of Silence.* London and New York : Zed Books.

Nathawat, S.S., & Mathur,A. (1993). Marital adjustment and subjective well-being in Indian educated housewives and working women. *The Journal of Psychology.* May. v. 127, n3, p353(6).

Obeyesekere, G. (1990). *The Work of Culture: Symbolic Transformation in Psychoanalysis and Anthropology.* Chicago: University of Chicago Press.

Panikkar, K.M. (1966). In *The Kama Sutra of Vatsyana.* W.G. Archer (Ed.). New York : Berkley Books

Parrinder, G., (1980). *Sex in the World Religions.* London : Sheldon

Pines, Ayala. (1999). *Falling in Love: Why We Choose the Lovers We Choose.* New York: Routledge.

Plummer, Kenneth. (1984). Sexual diversity: a sociological perspective. In K. Howells (ed.), *Sexual Diversity.* Oxford:Blackwell.

Puri, Jyoti.(1999). *Woman, Body, Desire in Post-colonial India: Narratives of Gender and Sexuality.* New York: Routledge.

Radhakrishnan, P., and Chan, D.K.S. (1997) Cultural differences in the relation between self-discrepancy and life satisfaction. *International Journal of Psychology.* pp. 32:387-98.

Raheja, Gloria., & Gold, Ann. (1994). *Listen to the Heron's Words: Reimagining Gender and Kinship in North India.* Berkeley: University of California Press.

Ramanujan, B.K. (1986). 'Social change and personal crisis: A view from an Indian practice', in M.I.White and S.Pollak (eds). *The Cultural Transition: Human Experience and Social Transformation in the Third World and Japan.* Boston: Routledge & Kegan Paul

Ramu, G. N. (1987). Indian Husbands: Their Role Perceptions and Performance in Single and Dual-Earner Families. *Journal of Marriage and the Family.* vol 49. no. 4. Nov. 1987, 903-915.

Rao, V.V. & Rao,V.N. (1982). *Marriage, the Family and Women in India.* Columbia, Missouri : South Asia Books.

Ratzlaff, C., Matsumoto, D., Kouznetsova, N., Raroque, J., Ray, R. (2000). Individual Psychological Culture and Subjective Well-being. In *Culture and Subjective Well-being.* E.Diener E.M.Suh. eds. (2000). Cambridge; MIT Press.

Reiss, I.L. (1986). A sociological journey into sexuality. *Journal of Marriage and the Family,* 48,233-242.

Roland, A. (1988). *In Search of self in India and Japan.* Princeton, NJ. Princeton University Press.

Roopnarine, J.L., Talukder, E., Jain, D., Joshi, P., & Srivastav, P. (1992). 'Personal well-being, kinship ties, and mother-infant and father-infant in single-wage and dual-wage families in New Delhi, India. In *Journal of Marriage and Family,* 54, 293-301.

______(1990). 'Characteristics of holding, patterns of play and social behaviors between parents and infants' New Delhi, India.' In *Developmental Psychology,* 26, 867-73.

Sacks, Karen (1992). Introduction: New views of middle-aged Women. In *In her prime: New Views of middle-aged women.* Ed. by Kerns,V. and Brown, J., 1-6. 2nd ed. Urbana: University of Illinois Press.

Satyam, Swamy. (1995,1997). *Happy Home; Vedic Sathya Sushma series.* Bangalore, India: Vedic Sathya Sushma Trust.

Schwartz, Pepper, & Rutter, Virginia. (1998). *The Gender of Sexuality.* Thousand Oaks,Ca:Pine Forge Press.

Seymour, Susan. (1983). "Household Structure and Status and Expressions of Affect in India". *Ethos* 11:263-277.

_________ (1993). Sociocultural Contexts: Examining Sibling Roles in South Asia. Pp. 71-101. In *Siblings in South Asia: Brothers and Sisters in Cultural Context.* Charles Nuckloss, ed. New York: Guilford.

________ (1999). *Women, Family, and Child Care in India. A World in Transition.* Cambridge, U.K.: Cambridge University Press.

_______ (1971). 'Patterns of child rearing in changing Indian town'. Unpublished doctoral dissertation. Cambridge, MA. Harvard University.

Sharma, Dinesh. (2003). *Childhood, Family, and Sociocultural Change In India: Reinterpreting the Inner World.* Dinesh Sharma (ed.). New Delhi: Oxford University Press.

Shukla, A. (1987). 'Decision making in single-and dual-caree families in India' in *Journal of Marriage and the Family,* 49, 621-29.

Shweder, Richard A. and Miller, Joan G. (1985). The Social Construction of the Person: How is it possible?. Pp.p.41-69. In *The Social Construction of the Person.* Kenneth J.Gergen and Keith e. Davis, eds., New York: Springer-Verlag. (Reprinted in Shweder, 1991.)

Sinha, J.P., and Verma, J. (1994). Social support as a moderator of the relationship between allocentrism and psychological well-being. In U.Kim, H.c.Triandis, and G.Yoon., eds., *Cross-cultural Research and Methodology: Individualism and Collectivism: Theory, Method, and Applications,* vo.18. Thousand Oaks.CA: Sage.

Srinivas, M.N. 1978. *The Changing Position of Indian Women.* New Delhi: Oxford University Press.

Sternberg,R.J. (1986). A Triangular Theory of Love. *Psychological Review,* 93 : 119-I,135

Suh, E.M. (2000). Self, the Hyphen between Culture and Subjective Well-being. In *Culture and Subjective Well-being.* E.Diener and E.M.Suh. eds. (2000). Cambridge: MIT Press.

Suh, E.M. and Diener. (1999). Self and the use of emotion information: Joining culture, personality, and situational influences. In *Culture and Subjective Well-being.* E.Diener and E.M.Suh. eds.(2000). Cambridge: MIT Press.

Suh, E.M., and Oishi, S. (2002). Subjective Well-being Across Cultures. In W.J.Lonner, D.L.Dinnel, S.A. Hayes, and D.N. Sattler (eds.). *Online Readings in Psychology and Culture (unit 7, chap. 10.* (http:// www.wwu.edu/culture). Center for Cross-Cultural Research. Western Washington University, Bellingham, Washington.

Tennov, Dorathy. (1980). *Love and Limerence : The Expression of Being in Love.* New York : Stein and Day

Thomas,W.I. (1966). The Relation of Research to the Social Process. In *W.I. Thomas on Social Organization and Social Personality.* Ed. Janowitz M. Chicago : University of Chicago Press.

Trawick, Margaret. (1992). *Notes on Love in a Tamil Family.* Berkeley: University of California Press.

Trianidis,H.C. (2000). Cultural Syndromes and Subjective Well-being. In *Culture and Subjective Well-being.* E. Diener and E.M.Suh. eds. 2000. Cambridge: MIT Press.

Vatuk, Sylvia. (1990). "To be a burden on others" : Dependency anxiety among he elderly in India. In *Divine Passions : The social construction of emotion in India.* Ed. by Owen Lynch, 64-88. Berkeley: University of California Press.

Uberoi, Patricia (1996). When is a marriage not a marriage ? Sex, Sacrament and contract in Hindu Marriage. In *Social Reform, Sexuality and the State.* Ed.P.Uberoi. New Delhi : Sage Publications.

Uberoi, Patricia (1993). Ed. *Family, Kinship and Marriage in India.* Delhi: Oxford University Press.

Wallerstein, J. & Blakeslee, S. (1995). *The Good Marriage: How and Why love lasts.* Boston: Houghton Mifflin Co.

Weeks, Jeffrey. (2003). *Sexuality* 2nd ed. New York: Routledge

Yelsma, P. & Athappilly, K. (1988). Marital satisfaction and communication practices: Compromises among Indian and American couples. Journal of Comparative Family Studies, 19, 37-54.

Zysk, Kenneth. (2002). *Conjugal Love in India: Ratisastra and Ratiramana.* Boston : Brill.

APPENDIX

The interviewees of this study were asked the following questions after informing them about the nature of the questions. They were also assured about the confidentiality of their responses and they were told that they are at liberty to refuse to answer any questions which they deem as too invasive.

ONLY the lead questions, not the follow-up questions are listed below. Follow-up questions were based on the answers to the lead questions, resulting in spontaneous and varied answers.

1. How did you meet your marital partner?
2. How long did you know her/him before you got married?
3. Were you engaged and How long were you engaged before you got married?
4. Did you go out during the period before the wedding to park, movies, restaurants ?
5. Did you write letters, call each other and exchange gifts during the period before the wedding?
6. How often did you see or meet each other?
7. Did you have a period of romance?
8. Were you sexually attracted to your partner when you met him/her for the first time?
9. Were you sexually attracted to him/her during the period of engagement or during the period of getting to know each other? When did sexual attraction begin?
10. Did you hold hands, kiss each other, caress or fondle ?
11. Did you have premarital sex?
12. Did you have good knowledge of sex before your wedding? Had you read *Kamasutra* ?
13. What premarital expectations did you have of your future husband/wife? In what they were realized or not realized (sometimes this question was

asked twice)

14. Did you have feelings of love for her/him during the period of getting to know each other
15. Did you fall in love with him/her during this time?
16. When did you begin to love your husband/wife? How long did it take to develop this?.
17. How do you define love?
18. Please tell me in explicit details about both the positive and negative experiences of your "first night".
19. Did you consummate your marriage on the first night? If not, when?
20. Was it positive? Did you enjoy ? Did you have a long foreplay? Was it a beautiful experience? Did you think it was a beautiful culmination of a long anticipation? or realization of your sexual expectations?
21. Were you a virgin? Were you pleased that she/he was virgin? How important it was for you that your partner was virgin or not?
22. What were some of your negative or unpleasant experiences of the "first night"?
23. Were you inhibited, shy, did you have pain or discomfort during sexual intercourse? Were you shocked to see the naked female/male body?
24. What surprised most about the sexual act?
25. Do you think your husband was under pressure to consummate the relationship on the "first night"? Did he force you or was he gentle and sensitive to you?
26. Was she sexually responsive to you and sexually excited ?
27. Did you experience orgasm the first time you had sexual intercourse ? When did you begin to experience orgasm? Describe your experience of orgasm.
28. Do you think presence or absence of sexual attraction to your partner before the wedding has an effect on the wedding night and sex life later on in your married life. If so, what kind of effect?

29. Do you think falling in love/being in love with your marital or not being in love with you partner influenced your "first night" experiences?
30. Tell me about your marital life in general and sex life **now** in particular? Are you sexually attracted to your husband/wife now? Do you have love and sexual satisfaction **now** ? or Was it there from the beginning of the marriage?
31. How do you rate your sex and marital life on a scale of 1-10.? Has it improved during your marriage?
32. How many times do you have sex? What priority does sex have in your married life?
33. Tell me about the different kinds of sexual practices you and your marital partner have. What kinds of sexual positions do you have? Which is your favorite? Do you have oral sex?
34. Do you make love in total nudity? With lights on?
35. Do you have sex on duty? Are you fully both physically and emotionally involved in love making ?
36. Tell me about your attitude towards sex. Has Hinduism created positive/ negative attitude towards sex?
37. Do you think Hindu wedding and "First night" rituals enhance or promote or hinder your sexual enjoyment? Do you think Hindu religion is a pro-sex religion ?
38. Did your family influence your attitude towards sex? Do you think Indian society is inhibited about sex?
39. What are the barriers to a healthy marital and sex life?
40. Do you think joint-family or extended family is beneficial to a good marriage. What are the problems and weaknesses of living with or close to an extended family?
41. What are the strengths and weaknesses of an arranged marriage?
42. If you were do it all over again, would you go through an arranged marriage or do you prefer to marry the person that you fall in love with ?

Index

T

U

V

W

Y

CPSIA information can be obtained at www.ICGtesting.com
Printed in the USA
LVOW102027060613

337280LV00002B/175/P

9 781842 901854